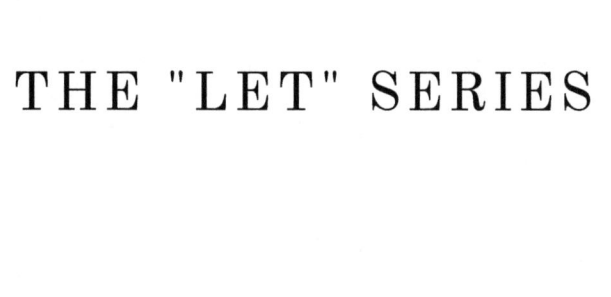

The "LET" Series

BECOMING A RESPONSIBLE CHRISTIAN

Anthony Adefarakan

GLOEM CANADA

THE 'LET' SERIES
Becoming A Responsible Christian

Anthony Adefarakan

Unless otherwise indicated, all Scripture quotations are taken from the King James Version of the Bible.

The "LET" Series
Copyright © 2022 by Anthony Adefarakan

Published by
GLOEM Publishing House
Calgary, AB, Canada
Email: info@gloem.org
Printed in Canada. All rights reserved.

No part of this book may be reproduced or transmitted in any form or by any means, electronic or mechanical, including photocopying, recording, or by any information storage and retrieval system, without permission in writing from the publisher, except for evangelical and/or spiritual education purposes only.

CONTENTS

Dedication

Preface

The "LET" Series

Why You Really Need Jesus

Become a Financial Partner with Jesus

About the Author

Other Titles by the Author and His Wife

DEDICATION

I dedicate this book to God Almighty for His goodness and faithfulness in making His Word available to me. All glory to His Holy Name.

Also to everyone desirous of a closer walk with God, living out Biblical Principles on a daily basis, I am in agreement with you; and I decree that the grace for a closer walk with God comes upon you now in Jesus' Name.

PREFACE

The 'Let' Series is a timely book, considering the times we are currently living in. Christianity is almost losing its true meaning as God's people no longer bother with instructions to obey from the Word of God as much as they bother with promises to claim. Our generation wants what God can give, but we are not interested in knowing Who He really is or what He expects of us as His children. That is why the Lord has laid it on my heart to write this piece as a reminder to all of us that we have certain responsibilities as God's children.

The word 'let' according to a dictionary implies allow, permit, cause or make; and it appeared in the Bible more than a thousand times. Whenever we see the word 'let' in the Bible, we are to pay attention because most of the time it is about to tell us what we can and should do. 'Let' shifts the focus from what God should do to what we should do simply because we can do it. And that is being a responsible Christian. It has been said that the faith that expects God to do everything for us is an irresponsible faith. God should only be expected to do His part when we have done ours; and that is what the 'LET' Series is all about: knowing and doing our part as responsible Christians.

So, kindly pay rapt attention to what the Lord will be revealing to you through this book and decide in advance to not only be a reader but also a doer, as the blessing is only in the doing.

As we consider some of these 'LET' statements, it is my prayer that the Lord will open your eyes and grant you perfect understanding as well as the grace for correct application in Jesus' Name.

"...let them make me a sanctuary; that I may dwell among them."
Exodus 25:8 KJV

According to this text, the Lord so much desires to dwell with His children not just for a day, a week, a month, or a year, but ALWAYS. He desires to protect you, to guide you, and to make His Presence available to you day and night. But first, He wants you to make Him a sanctuary (a dwelling place).

Create a sanctuary in your heart and let God become the center of all you do. Stop living your life as if you are in charge. Make Him the Lord and Controller of your life and affairs. Submit yourself totally to Him. If you do that, you will never lack His Abiding Presence all the days of your life. And remember, it is His Presence that makes the difference, not your sweat.

"...let them have dominion..."
Genesis 1:26 KJV

One of the paramount thoughts on the mind of God when He created man (including you) in His image was that man would dominate every other thing He had made.

Your destiny in God is to have dominion; to have absolute control over situations, circumstances, plants, animals, the cosmic world, etc.

Don't be dominated by what you were created to dominate. Find your place in Christ Jesus and start exercising your God-given dominion. It is a responsibility.

"...Let there be no strife...for we be brethren."
Genesis 13:8 KJV

Strife implies angry or bitter disagreement over issues. The Word of God says it should not happen among us as God's children because we are brethren.

Christians should not be found suing one another (dragging one another to court over disagreements); brethren should not be fighting over property, and church ministers of course should not be engaging in bitter disagreements over doctrinal or other church related issues.

The Word of the Lord clearly states: *"LET THERE BE NO STRIFE"*. And that means it is not beyond your power.

"...let him bring it, an offering of the LORD..."
Exodus 35:5 KJV

When it comes to giving an offering to the Lord, certain principles need to be applied. Your offering has to be BROUGHT to the Lord out of a willing and cheerful heart. The earlier part of that verse says *'whosoever is of a willing heart.'*

It must never be out of compulsion, coupled with grumbling, murmuring, and complaining. God is not a Forceful Collector. 2 Corinthians 9:7 says *'Every man according as he purposeth in his heart, so let him give; not grudgingly, or of necessity: for God loveth a cheerful giver.'* God loves a cheerful giver, and His reward is for those who honor Him with their offerings.

"...Let nothing, I pray thee, hinder thee..."
Numbers 22:16 KJV

Hindrances are those things that are still keeping you away from your goals and the fulfillment of your dreams. They may come in form of spiritual forces, financial difficulties, sicknesses, wrong relationships, and the likes. Their ONLY job is to make sure you don't reach your goal.

But the Word of God says *'let nothing hinder thee'*. So, what goals have you set for yourself, your family, career, business, or ministry? Arise, and go for them; let nothing (including the current situation in the world) hinder you. You are a winner every day!

"...let not your hearts faint, fear not, and do not tremble, neither be ye terrified..."
Deuteronomy 20:3 KJV

Fear is a killer. Most times, sicknesses and diseases don't kill as much as the fear they create. Fear can bring about High Blood Pressure, Nervous Breakdown, Heart Failure as well as Impulsive and Rash Detrimental Decisions, all of which can lead to untimely death.

Regardless of what is happening around you and regardless of the death figures you hear or see in the news, the Word of God says *'LET NOT YOUR HEARTS FAINT'*. Why? Your Keeper does not sleep nor slumber, and He is well able to keep all these evil happenings away from you (provided you have made Jesus your Lord and Saviour).

Be strong, you are heavily protected!

"...let your children know..."
Joshua 4:22 KJV

There have been times when things became so tough, but God came to your rescue. The Lord says *'let your children know'*. The things you now have and enjoy are the very things you used to pray about years ago. The Lord says *'let your children know'*.

God wants to be remembered as a Faithful God in all generations, hence He wants you to let your children know how good He has been to you. Psalm 145:4 KJV says *'One generation shall praise thy works to another, and shall declare thy mighty acts.'*

Let your children know...

"...Let us now prepare to build us an altar..."
Joshua 22:26 KJV

An altar is a place of meeting between God and man, and it doesn't necessarily have to be in a Church building. Your altar may be in your house, office, car, or simply a place in your heart that you have carved out or cultivated for meeting with God.

It is however worthy of note that altars don't just erupt or occur, they have to be built. You must consciously make the effort or prepare to build an altar to the Lord to keep His Abiding Presence with you always.

Have you built one?

"...let your hands be strengthened..."
2 Samuel 2:7 KJV

Just because you tried something last year and it didn't work doesn't mean it won't work this year. Unfulfilled dreams and unrealized goals have a way of weakening one's hands, thereby draining the energy to try again.

But the Lord is telling you today, *'let your hands be strengthened'*. Go back to where you failed and give it another shot. You are destined to win this season in the Name of Jesus.

"...let not arrogancy come out of your mouth: for the LORD is a God of knowledge..."
1 Samuel 2:3 KJV

Words usually reveal the true state of the heart. Jesus said, *'...out of the abundance of the heart the mouth speaketh.'* – Matthew 12:34 KJV.

If you are humble, your words will reveal it and if you have pride or arrogance in you, your words will equally reveal it.

Proverbs 16:18 says *'Pride goeth before destruction, and an haughty spirit before a fall'*. Get rid of every thought that makes you feel you are better than others. Such thoughts are very destructive. The admonition of the Lord to you today is "NEVER SPEAK ARROGANTLY".

"...let us return..."
1 Samuel 9:5 KJV

What is it that you used to do for God but no longer do because of tight schedules, busy jobs, marriage, overwhelming parenting, depression, acquisition of academic degrees, socio-political factors, church titles, or even increased financial status? Hear ye the Word of the Lord: RETURN.

Why? Jesus said in Revelation 2:4-5 NIV: *'...I hold this against you: You have forsaken the love you had at first. Consider how far you have fallen! Repent and do the things you did at first. If you do not repent, I will come to you and remove your lampstand from its place.'* God Have Mercy! Friends, *'...let us return...'*

"...let me go and pay my vow, which I have vowed unto the LORD..."
2 Samuel 15:7 KJV

A vow is a solemn promise, pledge, or personal commitment made to God. The moment you make a promise to God, you have a vow to fulfill.

It is however unfortunate that many people vow but refuse to pay. They vow when things are difficult, but the moment they become relieved, they forget about the vow completely. Now, that is a dangerous thing to do. Ecclesiastes 5:4-6 says it is better not to vow than to vow and not pay it. It further says refusing to pay one's vows could result in God destroying the works of one's hands.

Note that God is the One to do the destroying, not the devil. And who can rescue you from God's Hands? Let us pay our vows unto the Lord.

"...Let me now run..."
2 Samuel 18:19 KJV

When it comes to pursuing your visions or going after your goals, it has to involve running. You can't afford to be walking or strolling towards your goals in life; there's no time for that. You've got to run. Goals are not yet goals until they are given timelines. Someone said *'the moment you set a timeline for your vision it becomes a mission'*.

In Habakkuk 2:2 KJV, the Lord said *'...Write the vision, and make it plain upon tables, that he may run that readeth it.'* Did you see that? The Lord wants you to run with your visions. This year is going again, are you running towards your goals or you are merely strolling?

"Let your heart therefore be perfect with the LORD our God, to walk in his statutes, and to keep his commandments..."
1 Kings 8:61 KJV

What is a perfect heart? A perfect heart isn't one that doesn't make mistakes, rather, it is loyal and absolutely committed to God and His cause regardless of oppositions, distractions, or even persecutions.

If you still consider ungodly alternatives when it seems the answers to your prayers are being delayed, your heart isn't perfect with the Lord.

Like Job in Job 13:15, you must be able to say *'Though He slay me, yet will I trust in Him...'* Having a perfect heart with the Lord isn't as difficult as it sounds. All it requires is your SINCERITY!

"...let men say among the nations, The LORD reigneth."
1 Chronicles 16:31 KJV

To reign is to be in control, to be in charge, and to have absolute dominion. Many things attempt to reign over us in life: economic hardship, stubborn sicknesses, wicked political rulers, greed, unreasonable employers, etc.

At times, these factors appear so big that we literally forget that our help comes from the Lord. Until you learn to magnify the bigness of your God above the bigness of your challenges, you will never be able to say *'the LORD reigns'*. Today, say to all your challenges *'MY LORD REIGNS'*, and watch your problems reduce in size.

"...let us hear...what he saith."
2 Samuel 17:5 KJV

James 1:19 says '*Wherefore, my beloved brethren, let every man be swift to hear, slow to speak, slow to wrath.*' This is a generation where everyone wants to speak without taking the time to listen. As a matter of fact, listening is fast becoming old-fashioned.

Yet the Word of God says hearing should precede speaking. The Lord has so many things He wants to share with you; will you be willing to hear Him out?

There are also times He will send people to you; will you be willing to hear what they have to say? Someone has said the reason God gave us two ears and one mouth is so that we can hear at least twice before we speak once. Think about that!

"...let them go..."
Judges 15:5 KJV

What does the Lord want you to let go of? Your past mistakes. Your guilt. Your bitterness and resentment. Your eagerness to revenge. Your anger towards your offender. Your fruitless efforts. Your immoral lifestyle. Your disappointment and depression. Your suicide thoughts. Your ungodly relationships, among other things encouraging negative thinking or negative emotions in your life.

Today, decide and *let them go.*

"...let thine heart be merry."
Judges 19:6 KJV

It might interest you to know that certain sicknesses may never come your way if only your heart can be merry.

To have a merry heart simply means to be joyful, and that doesn't depend on the happenings around you. It's being joyful by choice.

Proverbs 17:22 KJV says *'A merry heart doeth good like a medicine: but a broken spirit drieth the bones.'* According to this scripture, every time you choose to be merry, you are eradicating conditions that may warrant you to be taking medications. It's that serious!

Choose a merry heart over a broken spirit.

"...let us fight against them..."
1 Kings 20:23 KJV

There are certain issues that constantly battle with our peace, joy, and healthy living. They include worries, anxieties, guilt, fear, etc. They are all enemies of our well-being.

How does the Lord want us to deal with them? Well, His Word says we should *fight against them*. Fight against your fear by putting your trust in God and fight against your worries and anxieties by resting in the Lord.

Stop tolerating these enemies in your life, *fight against them* until your joy is full. You are a winner in Jesus' Name.

"...let fire come down from heaven, and consume thee..."
2 Kings 1:10 KJV

Fire is a very faithful messenger. All you need to do is introduce it to what it needs to burn, and the rest is history.

Elijah was having a nice time in God's Presence when some soldiers sent by an evil king approached him to arrest him. Now, instead of going down to meet them, he told fire to attend to them, and in a moment, they all became ashes. Psalm 97:3 says fire goes before the Lord to consume all his enemies round about.

What is troubling your peace? What is disturbing your joy? What is threatening your fellowship with God? Go ahead and ask the fire of God to attend to them. Instead of coming down, *let fire come down*.

"...let the heart of them rejoice that seek the LORD. Seek the LORD and his strength, seek his face continually."
1 Chronicles 16:10-11 KJV

Seeking wealth will never cause your heart to rejoice.
Seeking marriage partners doesn't necessarily guarantee a joyful heart.
Seeking the fruit of the womb doesn't always cause the heart to rejoice as well.

To constantly have a rejoicing heart, you must seek the Lord. God is the Sole Giver of joy, and making His pursuit your priority makes a joyful heart inevitable. Determine to seek the Lord, and other good things of life will seek you (Matthew 6:33).

"...let the fear of the LORD be upon you..."
2 Chronicles 19:7 KJV

Isaiah 8:12-13 KJV says *'Say ye not, A confederacy, to all them to whom this people shall say, A confederacy; neither fear ye their fear, nor be afraid. Sanctify the LORD of hosts himself;and let him be your fear, and let him be your dread.'*

As a child of God, you are forbidden to fear what the heathen fear. No economic situation or health crisis should make you afraid. If you fear what they fear, you will suffer what they suffer.

Only ONE TYPE OF FEAR IS ALLOWED IN YOUR LIFE: THE FEAR OF GOD (which always results in deep reverence for God). Is the Lord ALONE your fear?

"...let us behave ourselves..."
1 Chronicles 19:13 KJV

Someone once said the two quickest ways to identify a fool are through their words and their behavior. And I will say, Christians can also be recognized by the same token.

As a child of God, you are an ambassador for Christ. People look at you and expect to see Christ in you - in the way you talk, work, behave, respond to issues, dress, and live generally.

With this consciousness, you are to live in a way that will not bring insults to the Name of Jesus. You are to represent Him with all dignity. That's what all Christians are called to do. How are you representing your Master? *Let us behave ourselves...*

"...let it be diligently done..."
Ezra 7:23 KJV

Anything you do for God must be diligently done. God notices and rewards diligence anywhere He finds it, and diligence simply means careful and persistent work or effort. Hebrews 11:6 says *'...he that cometh to God must believe that he is, and that he is a rewarder of them that diligently seek him.'*

That means God doesn't just reward everyone who seeks Him; rather He rewards those who DILIGENTLY seek Him. Proverbs 22:29 says *'Seest thou a man diligent in his business? he shall stand before kings; he shall not stand before mean men.'* God makes sure those who are diligent don't remain ordinary; He makes them stand before kings (like He did for Joseph in Pharaoh's palace).

What has the Lord put in your hands? Ministry, family, business, or career? Do it DILIGENTLY!

"...let judgment be executed speedily..."
Ezra 7:26 KJV

Are you in a position with legal authority to declare people guilty or innocent? If yes, then let justice be served speedily without fear or favor.

Proverbs 24:23-24 NIV says *'...To show partiality in judging is not good: Whoever says to the guilty, "You are innocent," will be cursed by peoples and denounced by nations.'* The Lord delights in righteous judgment because He is a Righteous Judge Himself.

Never deny the poor justice due to them just because they are poor and helpless. The Lord closely supervises every case being judged on the earth and it will be good for you to remember that He can still kill and make alive depending on where you stand. *Let judgment be executed speedily!*

"Let the people praise thee, O God; let all the people praise thee. Then shall the earth yield her increase; and God, even our own God, shall bless us."
Psalm 67:5-6 KJV

Did you know the earth responds when people praise God? Paul and Silas praised God and the earth quaked, bringing about their release from captivity (Acts 16:25-26).

Our text also confirms this. It says the earth will yield her increase when people praise God. Do you know why? It's because the earth is the Lord's and the fullness thereof (Psalm 24:1).

Everything you need and will ever need comes from the earth: food, water, building materials, gold, silver, diamond, natural gas, materials for printing money, etc. If you want the earth to release these things to you, you've got to learn to praise God not only on Sundays but as a lifestyle.

"...let all that be round about him bring presents unto him that ought to be feared."
Psalm 76:11 KJV

We go to birthday parties and present gifts to the celebrants.

We go to wedding ceremonies and present gifts to the newly wedded.

But when it comes to giving to God, we give Him explanations on how hard the times are and that He should please understand.

The Bible says you should bring presents to the Lord. Considering everything He has done for you and all that He's still planning to do, He deserves some presents.

"Let us come before his presence with thanksgiving..."
Psalm 95:2 KJV

Every door responds to its key. In the same way, the throne of God only grants access to those who use the right access codes.

Regardless of what you are facing in life, the Word of God says you must still come before the throne of your Heavenly Father with thanksgiving; not with lamentations, murmuring, and complaining.

Now, God wants you to be free with Him. He wants you to express how you feel, BUT that will be after your thanksgiving.

Psalm 100:4 TPT says *'You can pass through his open gates with the password of praise. Come right into his presence with thanksgiving. Come bring your thank offering to him and affectionately bless his beautiful name!'* Do you want God's attention this season? Engage the CORRECT PASSWORD.

"...let all the people say, Amen..."

Psalm 106:48 KJV

'Amen' simply means 'so be it'. When you say 'amen' to God's Word or declaration concerning your life, you are simply asking God to fulfill His Word in you. Mary was a virgin; but after the angel delivered God's message of supernatural conception and birth to her, she said *'...be it unto me according to Your Word...'* and she became the mother of our Lord Jesus Christ (Luke 1:38).

Despite all contrary factors, Mary said *'Amen'* and her life was transformed forever. What has the Lord told you? What Word has He sent to you? Will you say *'Amen'* as Mary did?

"...Let us rise up..."
Nehemiah 2:18 KJV

This is a call to action.
Let us rise up and take what belongs to us in Christ Jesus.
Let us rise up and put an end to all forms of satanic assaults in our lives.
Let us rise up and fight for what we believe to be true according to the Word of God.
Let us rise up and take our rightful place in Redemption.
Let us rise up and say 'No' to sin, carnality, ungodliness, and all forms of wickedness.
Let us rise up and fulfill the work the Lord has committed into our hands.
In what areas do you need to rise up today? Go ahead and take action.

"...let them not turn again to folly..."
Psalm 85:8 KJV

When we confess and forsake our sinful ways, God in His mercy and faithfulness forgives us and remembers our sins no more.

However, He expects us to remain loyal to Him by not returning to our old ways. During the earthly ministry of Jesus, it was not uncommon for Him to say *'Go and sin no more'* whenever He forgave and healed sinners.

If you are in Christ Jesus, your sins are forgiven. But there is a caution attached: DO NOT RETURN TO YOUR FOLLY!

"Let not mercy and truth forsake thee: bind them about thy neck; write them upon the table of thine heart: So shalt thou find favour and good understanding in the sight of God and man."
Proverbs 3:3-4 KJV

Do you want to be favored by God and man? Practice mercy and truth as a lifestyle.
Don't ever be without them at any point in time.
Favor will locate you.
The scriptures cannot be broken!

"...Let thine heart retain my words: keep my commandments, and live."
Proverbs 4:4 KJV

The reason some people commit sins is not because they do not hear the Word of God, rather, it's because they do not retain God's Word in their hearts.

In Psalm 119:11 KJV, the Psalmist didn't say 'Thy word have I heard that I might not sin against thee.' Rather, he said *'Thy word have I hid in mine heart, that I might not sin against thee.'* He had to retain the Word in his heart.

The wages of sin is (still) death (Romans 6:23 - Emphasis mine), and the only way to avoid it is to RETAIN THE WORD OF GOD IN OUR HEARTS so we can obey His commandments and live.

"Let thine eyes look right on, and let thine eyelids look straight before thee."
Proverbs 4:25 KJV

Distraction is one of the most potent tools the devil uses to capture his victims. If he fails at getting you through his lies (deception), he will engage distraction by simply shifting your focus away from your goals.

Someone once said the best way to get rid of a man's vision is to give him another vision. The moment he attacks you with distraction, you will suddenly discover that your ability to concentrate begins to diminish, and instead of staying focused, you may soon find yourself pursuing other things.

In John 6:15 the devil tried to distract Jesus, but He stayed focused: *'When Jesus therefore perceived that they would come and take him by force, to make him a king, he departed again into a mountain himself alone.'* Do what Proverbs 4:25 says, and you will reach your goal.

"...let all thy ways be established."
Proverbs 4:26 KJV

Multi-tasking is good, as long as it doesn't breed confusion. To establish your ways means clearly defining your tasks, decisions, and methods.

You can't afford to live in confusion. If you are suddenly asked what your reasons are for doing certain things, you should be able to clearly explain why. That's having your ways established.

Why are you doing what you are doing? Have you ever asked yourself?

"Let the saints be joyful in glory: let them sing aloud upon their beds. Let the high praises of God be in their mouth..."
Psalm 149:5-6 KJV

How does the Lord want us to go to bed?
With worries and anxiety about what tomorrow will bring?
With disappointment about unrealized goals for the day?
With the fear of nightmares or attacks during the night?
With thoughts of hopelessness or despair?
NOT AT ALL.

The Word of God says we are to sing upon our beds. We must go to bed full of gratitude for the day we just ended and also for the new day ahead. That's how to sleep and wake up in peace. And that's the way the Lord expects it to be. Never take your worries to bed!

"...Let us go into the house of the LORD."
Psalm 122:1 KJV

When you hear invitations like the one in the text above, how do you respond? Do you feel like you are being disturbed when someone invites you to Church, Bible Study Meetings, Prayer Meetings, and the likes?

If that's the case without any genuine reason, you are gradually losing your love for your Maker.
If you love God, you will love His House.
If you love God, you will love His Word.
If you love God, you will love His people.

The Psalmist said he was glad when they invited him into the house of the Lord. Is that your attitude also?

"...Let us go into the house of the LORD."
Psalm 122:1 KJV

Some people invite others to parties.
Some people invite others to clubhouses.
Some people invite others to cults.
Some people invite others to investments.
Some people invite others to movies.
And some people, like the Psalmist, invite others to God's Presence.

Since you have been worshiping in your Church, and since you have been attending those life-transforming programs, HOW MANY PEOPLE HAVE YOU INVITED?

Inviting people to other places but never to where they can meet with God and be blessed is not befitting for a Kingdom Ambassador! Think about that.

"Let the redeemed of the LORD say so..."
Psalm 107:2 KJV

Let the redeemed of the LORD say what? That they are redeemed. You see, if you claim you believe something but do not confess it, you don't actually believe it. Whatever you believe must be declared. 2 Corinthians 4:13 says *'...I believed, and therefore have I spoken...'*

So, are you saved? Say so. Are you healed? Say so. Are you delivered? Say so. Are you blessed? Say so. Are you prosperous? Say so. Are you anointed? Say so. Are you free? Say so. Are you successful? Say so. Whatever it is that you believe about yourself, especially as declared by the Word of God, start saying so in the Name of Jesus.

"...let thine heart keep my commandments: For length of days, and long life, and peace, shall they add to thee."
Proverbs 3:1-2 KJV

When it comes to keeping the commandments of God, our minds (not necessarily the devil) have always been the problem.

We think about them, rationalize them, analyze them and simply conclude that they don't make sense. And that's very true; because most of the things you will find in God's Word do not appeal to the senses.

That's why our text says to keep the commandments with our hearts because that's the only place it can be done. The mind questions while the heart simply believes. If you are really interested in pleasing God, relate more with Him and His Word using your heart. Then, let your heart educate your mind to comply. That's how you will receive the length of days, long life, and peace that He promised.

"Let not thine heart envy sinners..."
Proverbs 23:17 KJV

There are times people appear to be getting away with their sins. They practice unrighteousness and it seems as if they are achieving their goals without any form of repercussion. Don't envy them, and don't copy their ways. It's a delusion.

Sin will always attract the divine penalty no matter how long it takes. Don't follow sinful ways. Don't envy your colleague who bribed his way to the top and got the promotion you both wanted. Trust in God's power to promote you without offering any bribe.

Sinners are not worthy of your envy; rather they should be pitied and helped because *'the wages of sin'* is still death (Romans 6:23).

"Let us walk honestly..."
Romans 13:13 KJV

There is nothing shameful or stupid about being honest. Sometimes, honesty will get you into trouble. I have seen someone who lost an opportunity to work and earn income simply because he was honest about a question he was asked. He felt bad about it, but he had pleased God just by choosing to be honest. Regardless of what may be the outcome, choose to walk in honesty.

If a door closes as a result, the God you have honored will open better ones for you. Honesty is still the best policy!

"...Let us go speedily to pray before the LORD, and to seek the LORD of hosts..."
Zechariah 8:21 KJV

Prayer was never intended by God to be our last resort, but unfortunately, that's the case with many of us. Prayer is not something you do when all else has failed; rather, it's what you do FIRST to keep things from failing. Our text says *'let us go SPEEDILY to pray before the LORD'*. That's the concept. Speedily.

God wants you to pray (talk to Him) before you start your day; not only when your day isn't going as planned. Pray FIRST, and pray always. Don't wait until things get pretty bad before you remember to pray. Check out Amazon.com for our book *"OPERATING THE SPIRIT OF PRAYER"* - by Anthony Adefarakan. It contains great truths about this subject of prayer and can help shape your prayer life as intended by God.

"...let it be written..."
Esther 1:19 KJV

The Lord wants you to write. So, what does He want you to write? The visions He places in your heart (coupled with your plans, goals, and objectives toward achieving them) - Habakkuk 2:2-3. The Words He speaks to you directly, through His Holy Spirit, through His Word (the Bible), through His Ministers, through circumstances, etc - Jeremiah 30:2. The Revelation He gives you concerning yourself and others (including His Church, families, nations, etc) - Revelation 1:19. His commandments - Deuteronomy 6:6-9, 17:18. His mighty acts and plans for generations to come - Exodus 17:14-16. The covenant(s) He makes with you and your household - Exodus 34:27. The songs He teaches you - Deuteronomy 31:19.

In summary, the Lord really wants you to write, so start writing today.

"Let the priests, the ministers of the LORD, weep between the porch and the altar, and let them say, Spare thy people, O LORD, and give not thine heritage to reproach, that the heathen should rule over them: wherefore should they say among the people, Where is their God?"
Joel 2:17 KJV

Any issue or condition in the life of a Christian that can make people ask 'Where is your God?' qualifies as a REPROACH.

And as far as the Lord is concerned, He expects His Ministers to weep and cry to Him in intercession until such reproaches are lifted.

So, Ministers, don't just be saying *'It is well'*, cry to God for a change of condition in the lives of God's people - especially the ones He has entrusted to you.

If you are reading this and there are such reproaches in your own life making people to ask 'Where is your God?', I command such reproaches to be rolled away NOW in the Name of Jesus. Joshua 5:9 KJV says *'...This day have I rolled away the reproach of Egypt from off you. Wherefore the name of the place is called Gilgal unto this day.'*

The Lord Who rolled away the reproach of Israel at Gilgal rolls yours away too in the Name of Jesus. You are FREE in Jesus' Name. Amen.

"...let the weak say, I am strong."
Joel 3:10 KJV

Your words play a highly important role when it comes to the operation of faith. The Lord said you shall have whatever you say (Mark 11:23), and Matthew 12:37 says by your words you shall either be justified or condemned.

You may truly feel weak, but you are not to confess it. What should come out of your mouth if you desire strength is *'I am strong'*. That way, strength will come to you and your feeling of weakness will give way.

In this Kingdom, you don't say what you don't want to see. Take note!

"...let not them depart from thine eyes: keep sound wisdom and discretion: So shall they be life unto thy soul...Then shalt thou walk in thy way safely, and thy foot shall not stumble."
Proverbs 3:21-23 KJV

It is a very wonderful experience to have a vibrant soul (will, intellect and emotions), full of wisdom and discretion towards handling life's affairs intelligently.

And how beautiful it is to be able to walk safely in this highly unsafe world and society without stumbling! All these are made possible only on ONE CONDITION: LET NOT THE WORD OF GOD DEPART FROM YOUR EYES.

Keep your focus on the Word and the Word will attract the good things of life to you, because *'by faith we understand that the worlds were framed by the Word of God'* - Hebrews 11:2.

Decide for the Word today!

"...let the people tremble..."
Psalm 99:1 KJV

'The Lord reigns, let the people tremble...' It is a very dangerous thing to become too familiar with God. Yes, God is loving, compassionate, gracious, and merciful. But He is also a consuming fire; the One Who killeth and maketh alive (1 Samuel 2:6).

He parted the Red Sea by the blast of His nostrils and drowned His enemies in it. He divided the Jordan River. He rained down fire on Sodom and Gomorrah because of their sins. He is the LORD! Don't get too familiar with God, you must worship Him in deep reverence.

"...let them sacrifice the sacrifices of thanksgiving, and declare his works with rejoicing." Psalm 107:22 KJV

When does thanksgiving become a sacrifice?
When everything looks contrary to your expectations.
When your faith seems not to be working.
When you are in lack and God seems to be far away.
When you are confused about the next steps to take in life and God seems to be silent.
When you cannot understand what's going on anymore.

These times and the likes are seasons of sacrificial thanksgiving. You thank God even when you don't feel like it and when it doesn't make sense to do so.

Why? God's INTEGRITY can be depended upon even when events seem contrary. And according to 2 Thessalonians 5:18 and Romans 8:28, as you give thanks nonetheless, God will cause all your experiences to turn out for your good.

Give thanks always, even if it has to be SACRIFICIAL!

"...let nothing fail of all that thou hast spoken."
Esther 6:10 KJV

When you make promises to God or even to man, the Spirit of God takes note. You are responsible for fulfilling your promises, whether it is convenient or not. Do not be someone who lacks integrity. God abhors it. *'Let nothing fail of all that you have spoken...'*

"Let your light so shine before men, that they may see your good works, and glorify your Father which is in heaven."
Matthew 5:16 KJV

Where is the best environment for shining? Right amid thick darkness. This world is full of darkness: murders, corruption, oppression, greed, robbery, infidelity, compromises, suicide, depression, etc. To really know all these are happening, all you need to do is turn on the news.

But as God's children living in this same world, we are called to shine our lights so bright that people will notice and glorify our Father in Heaven.

How? For instance, when everybody is lying, decide to say the truth. When everybody is coming late to work, decide to show up on time. When everybody is cheating, choose to be fair. This way, you will be shining your light before men. Receive grace to do so in Jesus' Name.

"...let him first cast a stone at her."
John 8:7 KJV

A woman was caught in the act of adultery and they brought her to Jesus for judgment. They were going to stone her to death.

Jesus lifted up His voice and demanded that whoever had no sin should cast the first stone at the woman. But they all went away convicted of their own sinful states.

Why do you keep pronouncing judgment on others when you know how much you need God's mercy yourself? Think about that!

"...let him sell his garment, and buy one."
Luke 22:36 KJV

Jesus said anyone who doesn't have a sword should sell his garment (clothes) and buy one. Why is the sword so important? It's the weapon that can determine your existence or destruction. The Bible says God's Word is the Sword of the Spirit (Ephesians 6:17). Without it, the chances of becoming a victim in the battles of life are so high.

Don't have a Bible? Sell (even your very clothes) and get one. That's Jesus' recommendation.

"Let all things be done decently and in order."
1 Corinthians 14:40 KJV

The God we serve is a God of order. He moves among His people more freely when they are decent and orderly.

You can't crave Divine Presence and keep spending your days in strive, conflict, disorderliness, and all manners of indecency. God doesn't dwell in such. The Word of God admonishes us to do all things with decency and in order. Will you?

"...Let not your prophets and your diviners, that be in the midst of you, deceive you..."
Jeremiah 29:8 KJV

God's standard remains firm, and He will always do what He purposes. Prophets are wonderful people and they are God's spokesmen. However, no prophet has greater authority than the Word of God.

If you are living in sin for instance, and your prophet doesn't discourage it but instead prophesies security and protection over your life, he is practically deceiving you. The Word of God says there is no peace for the wicked and it also says the wages of sin is death.

So, listen to your prophets, but make sure everything they tell you is in line with the Word of God. If their prophecies go against the Word of God, reject them and go with the Word, because it is only the Word that is forever settled in Heaven (Psalm 119:89).

May you never become a victim of deception in Jesus' Name.

"...let us exalt his name together."
Psalm 34:3 KJV

Brethren, regardless of the state of our nations as far as the economy, security and politics are concerned, we are not called to lament, complain, grumble or murmur about them.

When we visit one another, the Lord does not expect us to keep discussing what is not working, rather He desires that His children will discuss what He is doing, like His provisions, protection, healing, divine assistance, favor, open doors, prevention from workplace accidents, etc.

That is the meaning of *'O Magnify the Lord with me, and let us exalt His Name together.'* When you go out this week, what are you going to discuss?

"...let this man be put to death...for this man seeketh not the welfare of this people, but the hurt."
Jeremiah 38:4 KJV

Which man should be put to death? Your FLESH. Why? It seeks your hurt, not your welfare. Your flesh is not your friend at all, in actual fact, it is your enemy. Your flesh doesn't want anything God wants for you. It is completely against the purpose of God for your life because it is that part of you that still takes instructions from the Adamic fallen state even when you are born again.

Your flesh wants extra-marital affairs even when it knows it's a sin. Your flesh wants to exhibit pride even when it knows such attracts destruction. Your flesh doesn't want to pray even when your spirit is willing. Your flesh, if not dealt with on time, could ruin your decades of ministry with just one error.

Stop responding to your flesh (carnal desires), it's like feeding a seemingly harmless cub (baby lion) that will later grow up and become wild enough to devour you. Put it to death NOW (by the Word of God and the help of the Holy Spirit). It's either you kill it or it kills you. There is no other way around it.

"...let not the dream...trouble thee..."
Daniel 4:19 KJV

Dreams have different sources. Sometimes God speaks to you through dreams, while at other times the devil takes advantage of your dreams to sow his plans. And according to Ecclesiastes 5:3, some dreams are mere results of your activities in the day.

Regardless of the nature of your dreams, DO NOT BE TROUBLED BY THEM. The Holy Spirit knows about all dreams regardless of their nature; learn to talk to Him in prayer for interpretation and plan of action instead of worrying about the dreams. *'...Let not the dream...trouble thee...'*

"...let him that thinketh he standeth take heed lest he fall."
1 Corinthians 10:12 KJV

Why did Samson fall? Overconfidence! Why did Peter deny Jesus? Overconfidence! Why did David commit adultery and murder? Overconfidence!

Nothing makes a man fall faster than the thought of being unable to fall. Just because you pray 25 times a day doesn't mean the devil will give you a break.

If the devil finds it difficult to use your weakness against you, he may decide to use your strength; and that's where overconfidence sets in.

Be very careful, no man is beyond falling. Only God can keep you standing, provided you are humbly doing your part. Take heed, lest you fall.

"Let this mind be in you, which was also in Christ Jesus: Who, being in the form of God, thought it not robbery to be equal with God: But made himself of no reputation, and took upon him the form of a servant, and was made in the likeness of men: And being found in fashion as a man, he humbled himself, and became obedient unto death, even the death of the cross. Wherefore God also hath highly exalted him, and given him a name which is above every name: That at the name of Jesus every knee should bow, of things in heaven, and things in earth, and things under the earth; And that every tongue should confess that Jesus Christ is Lord, to the glory of God the Father."
Philippians 2:5-11 KJV

That's the Jesus you are called to follow and emulate. How well are you operating with His kind of mind?

"...Let all things be done unto edifying."
1 Corinthians 14:26 KJV

To edify means to build up. When you speak, is somebody being built up or they are being torn down? When you write your reports, is somebody being built up or they are being torn down? Are your actions at work, in church, or in your neighborhood edifying? These are the questions you need to ask yourself if you are a child of God.

This is because GOD WANTS EVERYTHING YOU SAY OR DO TO BUILD OTHERS UP. *'...Let all things be done unto edifying.'*

"Let no one seek his own, but each one the other's well-being."
1 Corinthians 10:24 NKJV

There is nothing wrong with self-love. You should desire a good life for yourself and work towards it. However, there is a more honorable way to live. That is living for the good and benefit of others. When your thoughts and actions are geared towards making life better for others, you are beginning to understand the love of God.

To really live as God's children, we must be devoted to seeking others' well-being, and not just ours. And the reward is so great.

You can't make life better for others and not live a better life yourself. You reap what you sow. What you make happen for others, God will see to it that people make happen for you too.

Start seeking the best for others, whether they deserve it or not; and you will never be able to keep God's best away from your life.

"...let us not be weary in well doing: for in due season we shall reap, if we faint not."
Galatians 6:9 KJV

Doing good sometimes doesn't yield instant rewards. Some good acts will only be rewarded in the future (sometimes, it's even your children that will enjoy the benefits).

But whether immediate or in the future, NO GOOD ACT WILL GO UNREWARDED. So, do not be discouraged. Keep doing good as a lifestyle, you shall be rewarded if you do not stop.

"...Let not thine hands be slack."
Zephaniah 3:16 KJV

To deal with a slack hand simply means to be lazy, indolent, slothful, and unwilling to work. It is a clear sign of spiritual irresponsibility to live without working. Praying, fasting, reading the Bible, and even attending Church services faithfully will never replace working with your hands.

Jesus said *'...My Father worketh hitherto, and I work'* (John 5:17). And Apostle Paul admonished that whoever will not work should not eat (2 Thessalonians 3:10).

There may not be enough jobs for everyone, but surely there is work for everyone. Do something with your hands, that's how to qualify for the blessing of God upon the works of your hands. If there's nothing in your hands, what will God bless?

Think about that!

"...let every man, wherein he is called, therein abide with God."
1 Corinthians 7:24 KJV

The first call of God upon any man is a call from sinful living unto righteousness. Jesus said *'...you must be born again'* (John 3:7). However, just because you surrender your life to Jesus doesn't mean you have to change your vocation or job (unless it is an unholy profession).

You don't have to become a Bishop, Pastor, or Church employee simply because you are now born again. The Lord wants you to remain in your profession and shine His light there. Wherever you find yourself, you are His ambassador, and He plans to reach more people in your sphere of influence through this means.

God needs engineers to reach more engineers. He needs doctors to reach more doctors. He needs traders to reach more traders. He needs politicians to reach more politicians, etc. Stay in your profession and shine His light for others to see.

"...let none of you imagine evil in your hearts...and love no false oath: for all these are things that I hate, saith the LORD."
Zechariah 8:17 KJV

To imagine evil in your heart means to plan to do what is not good whenever the opportunity presents itself. This could be against yourself, your neighbors, employees, employer, family members, co-workers, city, nation, government, or even your place of worship.

Hardly does anyone carry out any evil plan without first imagining it. It all starts from evil thoughts. For instance, you can't commit suicide or genocide without first thinking about it.

Eradicate evil thoughts and imaginations from your heart and do not be involved in bearing false witness. The Lord says He hates these things. And if He hates them, you shouldn't expect Him to be happy with those who are involved in them. Hate what God hates, that's the pathway to living a godly and peaceful life.

> **"Let your moderation be known unto all men. The Lord is at hand."**
> **Philippians 4:5 KJV**

Moderation!!! This is a very important virtue all of God's children should strive to embrace as a lifestyle. It has been said that *'excess of anything is not good'*. Did you know that as refreshing and important as water is, if moderation is not employed in its consumption, it could lead to death?

The Lord wants you to be moderate in your dressing, in your speech, in your eating and drinking, etc. Yes, you are allowed to dream and think big, but don't let your desires get out of hand and turn into lust. That will be against the Law of Moderation. The Lord bless you with this virtue in Jesus' Name.

> **"...let him do it as of the ability which God giveth: that God in all things may be glorified through Jesus Christ..."**
> **1 Peter 4:11 KJV**

God made you and He knows the specific abilities He has endowed you with. To perform below your capacity or trying to perform beyond your abilities is not what He has called you to do. Rather, He wants you to do everything He has called you to do ACCORDING TO THE ABILITY HE HAS GIVEN YOU.

For instance, the Lord wants you to give offerings. But He doesn't expect you to give $1million when all He has blessed you with is $10000.

Also, if all the Lord has blessed you with is the ability to teach His Word, He doesn't expect you to start traveling from one country to the other, organizing and performing at Choral Concerts (when He hasn't given you such abilities).

What has God given you the ability to do? Get busy with that, while you leave the other things to those He has called to do them. That's what gives Him glory!

"...let your conversation be as it becometh the gospel of Christ..."
Philippians 1:27 KJV

Words are very powerful. Once spoken, they can't be retrieved. There is a way the people of the world (natural men) speak and there is a way the people of the Kingdom (Christians) are expected to speak.

As representatives of the gospel of Jesus Christ, our words are expected to be gracious, seasoned, and wholesome; not derogatory or damaging.

When you speak to yourself or others, your words should be healthy to the ears. Don't talk like everyone else in the world; talk like someone who has been entrusted with the gospel of Jesus. That's God's admonition to you through this text!

"...let the dead bury their dead."
Matthew 8:22 KJV

At some point in Jesus' earthly ministry, He told one of his disciples to follow Him while leaving the burying of the dead to the dead.

By this Jesus was implying that traditional, customary, or mundane activities SHOULD never be given priority over our SPIRITUAL ASSIGNMENTS.

For instance, as a child of God called to carry out the Great Commission, attending a traditional festival in your village should never replace participating in a Gospel Crusade. Following Jesus shouldn't be when everything else has been attended to, it is PRIORITY. Let those who have no life of Christ in them (the dead) attend to *'burying the dead'* while you get busy with your LORD.

"...Let us pass over unto the other side."
Mark 4:35 KJV

Jesus had been attending to the multitude, meeting their needs, and solving their problems. Then, suddenly He announced to His disciples, *'...let us pass over unto the other side'.*

Jesus knew that no matter how great your level of success is, there is still more on the other side. He didn't allow His current success to prevent Him from enjoying greater successes.

For instance, it was on His way to the other side that He spoke to the raging sea and it was calm to the amazement of His disciples. It was on the other side that He cast about 6000 demons out of a maniac whom no one could handle. It was also on the other side that He cured a woman who had been bleeding for 12 years and even raised Jairus' daughter from the dead.

A lot is waiting for you *'on the other side'*. Don't let your current success prevent you from enjoying greater ones. It's time to *pass over unto the other side.*

"Let all your things be done with charity."
1 Corinthians 16:14 KJV

If charity (or love as other renditions describe it) characterized our thoughts, words, and actions, the world would be a better place.

If love is in place, there will not be spousal infidelity, terrorism, gossiping, slanders, libel, business cheating, examination malpractices, hate speeches, eagerness for revenge among other ungodly behaviors and actions.

God wants love to be the motivation for all our actions. Why? Because He is LOVE (1 John 4:8). So, ask yourself, why do you do what you do?

"Let not sin therefore reign in your mortal body, that ye should obey it in the lusts thereof."
Romans 6:12 KJV

When sin is allowed to have its way in one's life, it graduates from 'once in a while' to 'reigning'. It simply begins to reign as king in such a life.

For instance, if you fornicate once and you refuse to confess and ask God for mercy, before you know what's happening you will become a slave to fornication. You will get to a level where it will seem as if you will die if you don't fornicate. At that level, it has entered the reigning phase in your life. And the same is true for every other sin.

Now, there is only one person who can prevent this from happening. And that person is YOU. Our text says DO NOT LET SIN REIGN IN YOUR BODY. If it's beyond your ability, God's Word will not say it's within your ability.

Do away with your sins (by the power in the Name of Jesus) before they become enthroned in your life. And if anyone is already reigning, dethrone them in Jesus' Name.

"Let us not therefore judge one another any more: but judge this rather, that no man put a stumblingblock or an occasion to fall in his brother's way."
Romans 14:13 KJV

Why do we judge one another as God's children? We judge those who don't speak like us; we judge those who don't dress like us; we judge those who don't celebrate the same holidays as us; we judge those who eat what we don't eat, etc. Yet we all call ourselves God's children.

Let us not judge one another anymore. God is the ONLY True Judge. Believe what you believe and give others the freedom to believe what they choose to believe as long as they too are God's children. You are free to correct those who err though or guide those who don't know better. However, let this be done in love. Stop judging people just because of doctrinal or denominational differences.

"...let the peace of God rule in your hearts...and be ye thankful."
Colossians 3:15 KJV

Once you surrender your life to Jesus, His peace becomes available to you. After that, it becomes your sole responsibility (with the help of the Holy Spirit of course) to ensure nothing takes away your peace. To lose one's peace is very easy; all it takes is anxiety. Being anxious, nervous, and unsettled will drain your peace any day. And the loss of your peace may result in the loss of your health.

Regardless of what is happening around you, guard your peace jealously. Don't give in to fear and worry (Philippians 4:6-7). And one way to do this is to learn to be thankful at all times (1 Thessalonians 5:18). You will not lose your peace in Jesus' Name.

"...Let us meet together..."
Nehemiah 6:10 KJV

The devil has one major strategy of luring God's children into his evil net of affliction and if allowed, destruction. And that is ISOLATION.

When he wants to deal with careless Christians, he starts feeding them with EXCUSES for not meeting together with other believers despite the Lord's admonition to do so in Hebrews 10:25.

Congregational attack is a very difficult task for the devil, he hardly has his way when believers meet together in unity. But the moment he can get someone out of fellowship, attacking such a fellow becomes so easy. Have you been giving excuses for not meeting with other believers in Church, Fellowship Meetings (online or in-person), Programs, etc? Watch out, an attack may be imminent.

Find a community of believers and start meeting with them. It's for your own good. And if you have been meeting, please don't stop. You will not suffer satanic attacks in Jesus' Name.

"Let him that is taught in the word communicate unto him that teacheth in all good things."
Galatians 6:6 KJV

The Lord has ordained that certain people teach His Word to demystify the truth contained in it, and this is a very great responsibility. They must do this as an assignment, and not for filthy lucre or profit-making. The Almighty God Who employed them to undertake this task is the ONLY ONE they must look up to for reward.

However, the Lord also commands that the recipients of such teachings should bless the teachers with all good things. If the Lord uses the teachers of His Word to bless you, it is your responsibility to bless them with anything good.

They are not to ask you for it, but you are to bless them with it. That's the Divine Order! May the Lord bless you with testimonies as you keep applying His Word in your life.

"...let us do good unto all men..."
Galatians 6:10 KJV

As God's people, one main reason the Lord saved our souls is to demonstrate the love of God to everyone down here.

He wants the world to experience firsthand what the love of God really means, and He has entrusted this great task to us.

The world will never know the meaning of God's love that led Jesus Christ to the Cross if all they get from us are anger, impatience, malice, bitterness, resentment, etc.

Let us do good to all men (regardless of race, tribe, ethnicity, religion, or beliefs); that way we will be shining the light of God in us, and everyone will notice that Christ indeed lives in us. May the Death and Resurrection of Jesus Christ never be in vain over our lives.

"Let no man beguile you..."
Colossians 2:18 KJV

To beguile is to cunningly deceive. Do not let anyone deceive you about the death and resurrection of Jesus Christ. He actually died on the cross, was buried, and resurrected on the third day for our justification according to the scriptures.

Do not let anyone deceive you that you can continue sinning since Christ has already paid for your sins. That's highly fallacious. Jesus paid for your sins so that you can have the power to say 'NO' to sin. Let the Word of God ALONE (and not some philosophical thoughts or theories) form the basis of your living. Jesus Reigns!!!

"Let us therefore come boldly unto the throne of grace, that we may obtain mercy, and find grace to help in time of need."
Hebrews 4:16 KJV

Jesus' Death and triumphant Resurrection opened the way for GRACE - unmerited favor. For those who believe in Him, it is no longer about what their abilities can accomplish but what God's grace can make happen for them. Do you need the intervention of Divinity in any area of your life? Get connected to the Resurrected Christ today. He's the Distributor of Grace. May His grace bring about the resurrection of every good thing that has died in your life.

"...let us also walk in the Spirit."
Galatians 5:25 KJV

Being born again means being born of the Spirit. Whatsoever is born of the flesh is flesh and whatsoever is born of the Spirit is spirit.

It is therefore contrary to the law of supernatural existence for anyone that is born of the Spirit to live and walk in the flesh. There's bound to be spiritual friction in such an existence.

So, are you born again? If yes, then you are not only expected to live in the Spirit, you are also expected to WALK in the Spirit - as a lifestyle. That is the nature of your new nature. Get on with it.

> **"...let us lay aside every weight, and the sin which doth so easily beset us, and let us run with patience the race that is set before us, Looking unto Jesus the author and finisher of our faith..."**
>
> **Hebrews 12:1-2 KJV**

No one runs well with a heavy load on their back. Loads are extra weights and they slow down movements. The race to heaven is a marathon, and it therefore calls for endurance. But to successfully run this race, two things must be in place.

Firstly, you must get rid of every weight of unhealthy habits, sinful relationships, works of the flesh, and any sin at all that you fall into easily (without thinking).

Then secondly, you must FIX your gaze on Jesus (not your Pastor or Bishop). He is the Author and Finisher of this race. He is the ONLY One Who can help you reach heaven at the end of this race.

> **"...let all those that put their trust in thee rejoice: let them ever shout for joy, because thou defendest them: let them also that love thy name be joyful in thee."**
>
> **Psalm 5:11 KJV**

Is everything going contrary to your expectations?
Are you almost becoming depressed because of unmet expectations and unfulfilled desires?
I have a question for you.
Is your trust in the Lord?
If yes is your answer, then rejoice.

God will defend you and He will fulfill your desires. So, you can as well start rejoicing now; because in verse 12, He promises to bless and favor you.

"...let thine eyes observe my ways."
Proverbs 23:26 KJV

There is a saying in the safety field: *'Stop, Think, Plan and Do.'* It is believed that if all workers practiced this, there would be fewer workplace incidents. And the same applies to our walk with God. We can't just live our lives anyhow. Jesus purchased us from Satan and sin by His own very precious blood. So, our lives MUST be deliberately lived to glorify Him.

That's why our text says to let our eyes observe His ways. Learn the way Jesus handled affairs when He walked on this earth and imitate Him in your own dealings as well. That's how to live to God's glory.

"...let him deny himself, and take up his cross, and follow me."
Matthew 16:24 KJV

Following Jesus is not a decision to be made based on emotional impulses. Just because you heard a very wonderful sermon or someone spoke to you so convincingly about Jesus is not sufficient reason for you to decide to follow Him. If you must follow Him, you have to count the cost and consciously decide to bear your cross while doing so. This is because Jesus doesn't just want to be your Saviour, He also wants to be your Lord. He wants to be in charge of every aspect of your life. And nothing short of total surrender is acceptable to Him.

So, are you a follower of Jesus or you are willing to become one? Don't just be emotional about it. Count the cost, deny yourself the authority over your own life, then carry your cross daily and follow Him. That's how to follow Jesus.

"Let the word of Christ dwell in you richly in all wisdom; teaching and admonishing one another in psalms and hymns and spiritual songs, singing with grace in your hearts to the Lord. And whatsoever ye do in word or deed, do all in the name of the Lord Jesus, giving thanks to God and the Father by him."
Colossians 3:16-17 KJV

Don't just read or hear the word of Christ, make sure it dwells in you richly. If you do that, coupled with the other requirements mentioned in the text above, you will be a worthy representative of our Lord Jesus Christ. And God will be glorified.

"...let your requests be made known unto God".
Philippians 4:6 KJV

Worrying, whining, lamenting, complaining, grumbling, and murmuring over your problems will never make solutions available to you. In fact, they will only compound them.

If you are genuinely interested in getting your problems solved, stop playing those nervous games mentioned above and start making your requests known to God. He's the Only One Who can solve your problems, and He has already promised to answer you when you call (Jeremiah 33:3). So, go ahead and tell Him about it.

"...Let no man despise thee."
Titus 2:15 KJV

To despise is to treat as insignificant or unworthy of notice. It means to disregard or count as unimportant. As God's children and representatives, the Word of God says you shouldn't allow this. Do not let anyone despise you or treat you as unimportant. Be confident, stand your ground and meekly declare what you know to be true (without getting involved in any strife).

Don't ever feel ashamed to stand up for the truth, regardless of who may get hurt. That's how Jesus lived. No man could shut Him down. He kept declaring His message until it was time for Him to leave for Heaven.

Lions are not known for cowardice. And you are the children of the Lion of the tribe of Judah. So, start behaving like one.

"...Let us not be desirous of vain glory, provoking one another, envying one another."
Galatians 5:26 KJV

When our collective tasks begin to have the 'our' attitude instead of the 'my' approach, things will get done easily. There is nothing wrong with succeeding as a team and then taking all the credit for the success together. But when one or two persons in the group set out to take all the credit to satisfy their desire for vain glory, there's bound to be strife, provoking envy and the likes.

Do not desire vain glory. Let your honor come from God. And be very okay with the credit not coming to you directly. It's virtuous to live that way.

"Let both grow together until the harvest..."
Matthew 13:30 KJV

It is no news that all manners of evil people surround us. And the unfortunate part is that they seem to be getting away with their evil enterprises.

Some of them rob workers of their due wages, kill breadwinners of families, oppress the poor and even attack whoever dares to help these helpless people. And they just seem to be having their way every time.

Beloved, do not be discouraged by this. Our Lord Jesus said before He left for Heaven that both evil and good people are allowed to *'grow together'* until the day of harvest.

On the harvest (judgment) day, every man shall get what they deserve – eternal punishment or eternal bliss. *'Behold, He is coming quickly and His reward is with Him, to give to every man according to their work'* - Revelation 22:12.

"Let your speech be alway with grace..."
Colossians 4:6 KJV

Jesus Christ spoke gracious words and He has called us to learn of Him, following in His footsteps. Luke 4:22 says *'And all bare him witness, and wondered at the gracious words which proceeded out of his mouth. And they said, Is not this Joseph's son?'*

Regardless of how people talk to you, and regardless of how hurt you are by people's actions, make it your goal to respond graciously. Not necessarily because they deserve it, but because God's Word says so. May the grace to do this rest upon us all in Jesus' Name. Amen.

"...let them that suffer according to the will of God commit the keeping of their souls to him in well doing, as unto a faithful Creator."
1 Peter 4:19 KJV

Nothing is interesting about suffering. It connotes pain, hardship, and the likes. If such comes upon you as a result of your own errors or actions, then you have no reward in view. The best you can do is learn from the experience and avoid such next time. That's it!

However, if you suffer as a result of your righteousness, or for the sake of God's Kingdom, *'blessed hath thou'*. You will be rewarded on earth and also in heaven.

For instance, you stood your ground against corruption in your place of work and you were set up, dismissed, and denied any severance pay. And this has brought untold financial hardship upon you and your family. Rejoice! Your suffering will not be in vain. Stay true to the Lord, He will compensate you for standing up against unrighteousness. Don't give in to evil. Rather suffer for doing God's will. Great is your reward.

"...let these also first be proved; then let them use the office...being found blameless."
1 Timothy 3:10 KJV

The Word of God says we shouldn't lay hands hastily on anyone. That is, we should never rush into ordaining anyone for ecclesiastical duties.

It is good to have the desire to serve in the House of God - as Deacons, Deaconesses, Pastors, Bishops, etc. But it is not just about desires, there's more to it.

If a wrong person is ordained, such a fellow could become a victim of the anointing. That's why the Word says they should *'first be proved'* and *'found blameless'* (without faults) before being ordained to handle spiritual offices.

What are the ordination criteria in your Church? Are you still doing it the way the Word says it should be done? Have these reviewed, please.

"...let us not love in word, neither in tongue; but in deed and in truth."
1 John 3:18 KJV

Anyone can say *'I love you.'* Why? Talk is cheap, and anyone can afford it. But to love is more of a demonstration than a statement. The Word of God says *we should not love in word or tongue but in deed and in truth.*

God wants us to be sincere about our love for Him and others, and He wants us to demonstrate it by the way we live and relate with Him and others.

How can we claim to love our neighbors when we close our eyes to their problems which we can solve? And even if we can't solve them, at least we can pray for them. God is looking for action-based lovers, not just love-announcers. Are you one?

"...let him glory in the Lord."

1 Corinthians 1:31 KJV

There are certain achievements and feats that one cannot help but talk about. There is nothing silent about great victories and achievements. And at this stage, the temptation to boast becomes so irresistible.

But here is what the Word of God has to say about such moments: *Let your boasting (glorying) be in the Lord.* Why? Because a man cannot receive anything (including those achievements) except he is given from heaven (John 3:27).

Be very careful about how you handle your moments of success and victory. They may turn to moments of sorrow if not handled the way God expects. If you don't believe me, ask Nebuchadnezzar. It took him 7 years of living like a wild animal for him to understand this (Daniel 4:28-37). Beware!

"...let him be your minister...let him be your servant:"
Matthew 20:26-27 KJV

As far as Jesus is concerned, leadership is all about service, not dominion. He said whoever wants to be the greatest should become a servant.

As God's children, the pattern of this world shouldn't dictate our conduct. We are representing a Kingdom down here, and in that Kingdom, those who serve others are considered the greatest. How are we fulfilling our leadership roles? Are we 'bosses' or servants?

"...let us not sleep, as do others; but let us watch and be sober."

1 Thessalonians 5:6 KJV

We don't need a prophet to tell us that this world is moving towards its end. All the foretold signs are around us already.

That's why this is the time to be as fully 'awake' as possible. We need to be 'awake' to holiness, love, kindness, forgiveness, watchfulness, ceaseless prayers, and the Great Commission as commanded by our Lord Jesus Christ. *Let us not 'sleep'* at this time.

We can't afford to be careless anymore. Our King shall soon return, and He must meet us fully 'awake'. Receive grace to be fully 'awake' in Jesus' Name.

"...let us therefore cast off the works of darkness..."
Romans 13:12 KJV

What are the works of darkness? Anything you do intentionally as a Christian that you know will bring you shame and embarrassment if others should know about it.

As a Christian, will you be so bold to watch internet or TV pornography in the presence of your church members? Or as a man or woman of God, how happy will you be if your congregation should find out that you still visit strip clubs, consume alcoholic drinks to the point of getting drunk, embezzle church funds and even masturbate when no one is watching?

All these and many more like them are SHAMEFUL WORKS OF DARKNESS. They are things we don't ever want to come to the light. But whether others know or not, God surely knows about them in detail, and He will one day bring those things to light. *Let us cast off the works of darkness;* you can't cast out the devil or stop his operations in your life if you still practice the works of darkness. He's the king of darkness. You can't avoid his influence unless you repent.

"...let your communication be, Yea, yea; Nay, nay: for whatsoever is more than these cometh of evil."
Matthew 5:37 KJV

Simply put, the Lord is saying: *'Let your Yes be Yes and let your No be No; do not say Yes when you mean to say No.'* If you cannot live by this simple principle in your daily affairs, Jesus Christ believes that some kind of evil is involved.

Don't be caught in the web of trying to give explanations when your answer should be Yes or No. Say No to fornication and adultery. Don't say *'my spirit is willing but my flesh is weak.'* Say No to Lies. Don't say *'well, it's not really a harmful lie.'* Say Yes to holiness. Don't say *'everybody is a sinner.'* Let your Yes be Yes and let your No be No. That's Jesus' expectation from you.

"...let not thy left hand know what thy right hand doeth:"
Matthew 6:3 KJV

In one of the teachings of Jesus, He mentioned God's expectation regarding our almsgiving and good deeds. He said *we shouldn't let our left hand know what our right hand is doing.*

The Lord wants us to do these things secretly without calling attention to ourselves. The whole world doesn't have to know that if not for your help, a poor widow somewhere would have died of starvation. That's a good act of course, but it shouldn't be a headline in the newspapers nor a trending story on social media.

When you do your almsgiving or give help to attract attention in order to receive the praise of men, regardless of your spiritual status or title, you have lost your reward from God.

'Do not let your left hand know what your right hand is doing' - that's the rule if you are interested in divine rewards.

"...let a man examine himself..."
1 Corinthians 11:28 KJV

If you do not examine your life, who will? Your life is like a vehicle; unless directed, it will run on its own - and will usually end up crashing. Examine your attitudes, habits, daily routines, income, expenditure, relationships, mindsets, driving, speech, body, health, career path, ministerial operations, spiritual growth, anxieties, worries, beliefs, prayer life, level of faith, parenting style, etc.

All these and everything else that makes up your life need to be examined and worked on from time to time. Life is work, and living is more work. Someone has said *'an unexamined life is not worth living.'* Examine yourself!

"...let not man put asunder."
Matthew 19:6 KJV

No man is permitted to divide or set apart what God has joined together, especially when it has to do with husbands and wives.

If you are in the habit of destroying relationships by your evil schemes, repent. Proverbs 6:19 says God HATES those who sow discord among brethren. If you belong to this category, you are operating under divine hatred which simply implies closed heavens. Repent today. Do not be an agent of division. Mind your own business.

"...let us be therewith content."
1 Timothy 6:8

Contentment is a state of happiness and satisfaction - which doesn't in any way depend on having all your desires in life fulfilled, but which actually comes from a heart that is grateful for the desires and necessities of life already granted.

As beautiful as contentment is, it's fast disappearing from our society. People no longer think about what they already have with gratitude simply because they are yet to get what they still want. And this has paved the way for greed, corruption, cheating, fraud, murder, etc.

Yes, God wants you to dream big. He wants you to ask Him for more. But He also wants you to be content with what you already have while waiting for the ones He will yet provide. Make contentment your goal this period, it's one of the greatest recipes for a peaceful life on this planet. *'But godliness with contentment is great gain.'* (1 Timothy 6:6 KJV).

"...let him speak my word faithfully. What is the chaff to the wheat? saith the LORD."
Jeremiah 23:28 KJV

Are you called to preach or teach God's Word? Do it faithfully. Are you called to give prophetic words from God? Say only what He says. You see, when delivering God's message, it's very possible to fall into the temptation of sharing our thoughts, opinions, beliefs, ideas, and even experiences with little or no emphasis on God's undiluted Word. That is like sharing chaff instead of wheat.

Only the Word of God can change people, not our views. Speak the Word of God FAITHFULLY (EXACTLY AS IT IS). Psalm 19:7 says *'The law of the LORD is perfect, converting the soul...'*

Do you want to see results in ministry? Suspend your own opinions and only dish out the Perfect Law of the Lord which is what converts souls.

"...let us put on the armor of light."
Romans 13:12 NKJV

We live in a world where darkness is not only tolerated but also celebrated. The wicked are awarded prestigious positions while the honest and righteous ones are relegated as unimportant in society. To therefore live safely in this kind of environment, we need to put on the armor of light.

Light is a weapon. It is both defensive and offensive in operation. The light of God upon your life can keep satanic forces away from you and can even slay those who try to come close. If you don't put on the armor of light by PRACTICALLY living according to the Word of God, you would not be able to resist the works of darkness going on in the world. Think about that for a moment!

"...let each one give as he purposes in his heart, not grudgingly or of necessity; for God loves a cheerful giver."
2 Corinthians 9:7 NKJV

God commands us to give (Luke 6:38), and He expects us to obey this command regardless of how we feel about it because it is one of the reasons He blesses us.

However, He doesn't want us to give grudgingly. In giving our time, advice, services, money, prayers, counsel, attention, recommendations, etc., God doesn't want us to complain, murmur, or grumble. He wants us to do these cheerfully because that's the only way we can be rewarded.

If what you want to give will involve grumbling or lamentations, hold on until you can do it without complaining. If God loves cheerful givers, it means He doesn't love those who give grudgingly. Think about that!

"...Let every one that nameth the name of Christ depart from iniquity."
2 Timothy 2:19 KJV

Christ is Holy. He's pure in character, speech, and works. There is nothing sinful about Him because He defeated sin and death at Calvary.

Now, if you claim you belong to Him but still indulge in iniquity of any kind, you really do not know Him; and you are dragging His stainless reputation in the mud. Get rid of all your sinful and carnal inclinations if you sincerely belong to Jesus. That's how to live without bringing shame to His Holy Name on earth and without hearing *'depart from me you workers of iniquity'* on the last day.

"...let us offer the sacrifice of praise to God continually, that is, the fruit of our lips giving thanks to his name."
Hebrews 13:15 KJV

Praising God requires no effort at all when everything is going as planned. When all your expectations are being met and everything seems to be working in your favor, you do not need any admonition to give praises to God.

However, when it looks as if all hell is let loose on you and nothing you touch seems to be working, will you still be praising God?

Well, there's something called the sacrifice of praise. It is the kind of praise you offer to God when it is most difficult to do so. Our text says we should offer this continually (regardless of what may be happening in and around us).

May the grace to obey this instruction rest upon us all in Jesus' Name. And as we do, may our situations change for good in Jesus' Name.

"Let all bitterness, wrath, anger, clamor, and evil speaking be put away from you, with all malice."
Ephesians 4:31 NKJV

This is clear enough for anyone to understand. *Bitterness, wrath, anger, clamor, malice, and evil speaking* are not permitted in the life of anyone who belongs to Jesus. If you know you still harbor these, do not excuse or explain them away. Talk to the Lord about them and receive grace to get rid of them in Jesus' Name. All will be well.

"...let us run with patience the race that is set before us, Looking unto Jesus the author and finisher of our faith..."
Hebrews 2:1-2 KJV

Christianity is a race, not a religion. And it is not a sprint or a dash; rather it is a marathon - with HEAVEN as its finish line.

The day you sign up to become a follower of Jesus, you get enlisted to begin the race to Heaven. Being a marathon race, it is a long haul; and there are many things you will have to endure while running. You will need to endure discouragement, distractions, false brethren, betrayals, persecution, moments of joy and sorrow, fulfilled and unfulfilled desires, etc.

The only way you can run this kind of race without falling out is to exercise patience and keep your focus on Jesus - the Author and Finisher of the race.

No matter what you face in this journey of Christianity, never lose sight of Jesus and His teachings. That's the only way to finish strong and well. You will not fall out in Jesus' Name.

"...Let us build..."
2 Chronicles 14:7 NKJV

In God's Kingdom, we are always building - with eternity as our focus. To not be involved in this building business as a child of God is to be stagnant, which is not permitted in the Kingdom.

What should you be building as a Christian? Your relationship with God. Have you grown in your walk with God between last year and now? Your fellowship with other brethren. Your patience and tolerance levels. Your discipline and self-control. Your ability and confidence to tell others about Jesus. Your faith and prayer life. Your Kingdom investments through giving. Your Word-level. Your spiritual stamina etc. God is a Builder Himself, and He expects His children to be builders too. *Let us build...*

"...let not your hands be weak: for your work shall be rewarded."
2 Chronicles 15:7 KJV

Have you been laboring so hard to ensure the organization you work for succeeds but it seems no one appreciates all your efforts?

Are you discouraged by how your Pastor, Boss, or even co-workers treat you despite your commitment, dedication, and faithfulness?

Are you on the verge of giving up on your good works because no one seems to be noticing? Or you have even been praying and making confessions of faith but nothing seems to be happening.

The Lord has sent me to you THIS VERY DAY with this message: *LET NOT YOUR HANDS BE WEAK, YOUR WORK SHALL BE REWARDED!* God doesn't miss any detail; He surely sees all you do. And your reward is coming from Him. Be encouraged; your reward is imminent.

"Let your heart therefore be perfect with the LORD our God, to walk in his statutes, and to keep his commandments, as at this day."
1 Kings 8:61 KJV

In Matthew 5:48, our Lord Jesus Christ says *'Be ye therefore perfect, even as your Father which is in heaven is perfect.'* God is perfect, and He expects His children to be perfect as well. Don't mind those who preach otherwise. God has spoken, and His Words are NEVER subject to man's editing.

That being said, whatever God expects of His children, He always provides the grace to make it happen. So, He doesn't expect you to be perfect on your own; rather He expects you to rely on His perfect power to achieve that. And that's why He sent Jesus to us as an Example we can follow in order to become all He wants us to be.

What then is your responsibility? Don't try or struggle to be perfect; just make sure your HEART is perfect with the Lord - that is, be loyal to the Lord and His Word WHOLEHEARTEDLY. Don't share God's place in your heart with anyone or anything else. God will use this loyalty of yours to bring about perfection in every other area of your life. Your heart is where the job gets done.

"...Let us flee..."
Judges 20:32 KJV

According to a dictionary, to flee means to run away from a place or situation of danger. Now, the Word of God commands us to flee from certain things. For example; we are to flee from God's wrath that is coming upon sinners (Matthew 3:7).

How? By accepting the Lordship of Jesus Christ over our lives. We are to flee from youthful lusts and fornication - sexual sins (2 Timothy 2:22 and 1 Corinthians 6:18). How? By total abstinence and RUNNING AWAY FROM ANYONE OR ANYTHING THAT CAN FUEL THE DESIRE.

We are to flee from idolatry (1 Corinthians 10:14). How? By RUNNING AWAY from anyone or anything that tries to replace God or contends with the place of God in our lives. These are just to mention a few.

Take note, the Lord didn't say stand your ground against them or resist them; rather He said RUN AWAY FROM THEM. Why? They can't be resisted; they can only be avoided. And if God (the One Who created you) says flee, please kindly flee.

"...let them go..."
2 Kings 2:16 KJV

You shared your vision with them and they started avoiding you. They won't even pick up your calls anymore. Let them go.

You can't get everyone to believe in your dreams. Jesus at one time shared His vision with His followers and many of them stopped following Him. But that didn't stop Him from fulfilling His purpose. What else should you let go of?

Your past successes. If you hold on too tightly to them, you may never record other ones. Give thanks for them, but let them go so that you can pursue other ones. There are several other people and things you need to let go of. Ask the Lord to show you whoever or whatever is holding you or slowing you down; and as soon as He shows you, simply *LET THEM GO!*

"...let us return unto the LORD..."

Hosea 6:1 KJV

In this Christianity race, falling is not as terrible and dangerous as refusing to rise after a fall. Peter denied Jesus at His hour of need. That was very bad. But he didn't remain in that state; he returned to the Lord in heartfelt repentance, and not only was he restored, he was also made the pillar of Christ's Church.

Do you feel you have disappointed God by something you said or did? Or by something you refused to say or do? Don't stay in that state. Repent and come back to the Lord for restoration. His arms are always wide open to welcome backsliders and lost sheep. Return to the Lord TODAY!

"...Let no one be missing..."

2 Kings 10:19 NKJV

When it comes to the salvation of your household and the worship of the Almighty God, no one is to be missing. The Lord doesn't just want to save you; He also wants your family members to be saved. That's His plan.

Cornelius in Acts 10:24 gathered his relatives and close friends to hear the words of salvation and the Lord saved his household. Also, the jailer in Acts 16:31-34 got saved together with his household.

What are you doing about the salvation of your family members and close friends? Are you talking to them about Jesus or you are just talking about politics and sports? God wants you to ensure they are saved. So, start praying for them; tell them about Jesus and expose them to platforms or programs that can help them believe. You will not lose your household to Satan in Jesus' Name.

"...let her be careful...All that I commanded her let her observe."
Judges 13:13-14 NKJV

Women are wonderful treasures to God, and He fulfills many of His plans on earth through them. Through Hannah's prayers, Samuel - one of the greatest prophets in Israel - was born. And through Mary's faith in God, Jesus - the Redeemer of all mankind - was born. The list goes on and on.

However, the devil fully recognizes their power of influence and he usually lures them to his side so he could work through them as well. And that's why he didn't go to Adam but went to Eve in the Garden of Eden. Also, he used Delilah to finish off the Samson that all the Philistines couldn't handle. God knows about this and that's why He wants you to be careful and observe all His commands as a lifestyle so that you will not become an instrument in the hands of the devil. Beware and observe!

"...let us make a covenant with our God..."

Ezra 10:3 KJV

To really enjoy your relationship with the Lord, you should enter into certain covenants with Him. Now, just by belonging to Christ, you are already a covenant child of His. However, there are other benefits associated with striking a deal with Him regarding different aspects of your life.

For instance, you can enter into a covenant of divine health with the Lord and never experience sickness again. All you need is to locate His Word on that subject and commit your life toward fulfilling the demand. Divine health will become yours by covenant regardless of what is going on around you. Covenant is stronger than a promise. Get into a covenant relationship with God today.

"Let all the earth fear the LORD; Let all the inhabitants of the world stand in awe of Him. For He spoke, and it was done; He commanded, and it stood fast. The LORD brings the counsel of the nations to nothing; He makes the plans of the peoples of no effect. The counsel of the LORD stands forever, The plans of His heart to all generations."
Psalm 33:8-11 KJV

If all the reasons above are not sufficient for you to fear God, then kindly explain to me how a man could be thrown into the den of hungry lions and still come out alive without any scratch.

Also, I will like to know how three men thrown into a blazing furnace could come out of the fire without any impact on their clothes or skin. Don't let anyone deceive you, there is no one like OUR GOD. And for that alone, HE MUST BE FEARED!

"...let the righteous be glad; Let them rejoice before God; Yes, let them rejoice exceedingly."

Psalm 68:3 NKJV

Why should the righteous be glad?
Because the Word of God says so.
Because their sins have been forgiven.
Because their names are written in the Book of Life.
Because they are partakers of the divine nature.
Because they shall inherit the Kingdom of God.
Because the Lord fights their battles and delivers them.
Because it shall be well with them.
Because their prayers bring God delight and He answers them.
The list goes on and on.

As believers, we are the righteousness of God in Christ Jesus, and our reasons for rejoicing far outweigh our reasons for complaining. Let us be glad in the Lord.

"...let down your nets for a catch."
Luke 5:4 NKJV

One major issue with failing is the lack of zeal to try again. That's why there are so many projects that have been left uncompleted.

But failure is never a destination, it's merely an event. And when your trust is in the God Who gives success, you haven't made your last attempt yet until you succeed.

In Luke 5, Peter fished all night and caught nothing. Now that's a failure. But at the instruction of Jesus Christ, he tried again and recorded an amazing result. You too can try again; success awaits those who refuse to give up.

"Let us search and try our ways..."
Lamentations 3:40 KJV

God doesn't just relate with us based on our words and actions alone, He also considers and carefully examines our motives. That's why for instance He could say He loves cheerful givers - not just givers, but cheerful givers. It's because He knows the states of our hearts, and He's moved more by that than our actual words and actions.

Now, since He knows the contents of all hearts, it will be wise for us to search and examine our hearts and get rid of anything that if found may be displeasing to Him. May your life continually bring glory to God in Jesus' Name.

"Let us lift up our hearts and our hands to God in heaven, and say: "We have sinned and rebelled..."
Lamentations 3:41-42 NIV

Nothing disrupts a man's fellowship with God more than sin. Sin is a divider. It blocks man's access to divinity and keeps him away from all that is good as ordained by God.

Are you feeling spiritually empty? Are you feeling some sort of disconnection from God? Is your peace gone? Those are signs of broken fellowship. Don't wait, do what the text above says and ask to be restored. The Lord will pardon you and get you back into fellowship. Do this without delay!

"...let none deal treacherously..."
Malachi 2:15 KJV

Treachery means betrayal of trust; deceptive action or nature; and the Lord doesn't want any of His children to be involved in such.

Cheating on your spouse doesn't portray you as a smart person; rather it portrays you as one who deals treacherously.

Betraying the trust your employer or leader has in you is also treachery. Treachery can cost you your very life. It's that dangerous. If you don't believe me, ask Judas Iscariot; he dealt treacherously and never lived to tell the story. He died shamefully. The Lord has spoken; *let none deal treacherously*. Obey in your own best interest.

"Let nothing be done through strife..."
Philippians 2:3 KJV

Strife implies angry or bitter disagreement, vigorous or bitter conflict, discord, or antagonism. That is a quarrel, struggle, or clash.

Why does the Lord want us to avoid strife? It's because according to 1 Corinthians 14:33, *God is not the author of confusion, but of peace.* And according to James 3:16, *where envying and strife is, there is confusion and every evil work.*

There can't be peace where there is strife - it doesn't matter if that's in your family, your place of work, or even your church.

God doesn't stay where there is strife. So, to do anything through strife or to be involved in such is to cause God's Presence to depart and as a result, encourage every evil work. Is that what you want? I believe you don't want that. Then, *let nothing be done through strife.*

"Let no man despise thy youth; but be thou an example of the believers, in word, in conversation, in charity, in spirit, in faith, in purity."
1 Timothy 4:12 KJV

God doesn't just call or choose the elderly for His Kingdom assignments; He uses the youths too. Samuel was a youth when he started hearing from God. David was a youth when he killed a lion, a bear, and even Goliath. Jeremiah was a youth when God called him and gave him an assignment. Timothy was a youth when he became a missionary. The list goes on.

God can use you for His glory; so, don't let anyone despise you or look down on you just because you are young. Be a worthy example of godly youths by your conduct and faith. Let your light so shine before men and bring glory to God by the way you live. God can do great things through you. Trust me.

"...Let every man be fully persuaded in his own mind."
Romans 14:5 KJV

The Word of God says whether people regard some days as more sacred than others or they simply treat every day alike, it doesn't really matter. What matters is being fully convinced in your own mind regarding this.

If you don't believe in Christmas, Good Friday, Easter, or the likes, it's your choice. Don't see those who do as ignorant or ungodly.

Those who treat those days with respect do so based on their own convictions as well. And they also have no right to criticize those who don't.

Let the way you treat each day the Lord blesses you with reflect your gratitude and respect. Honor each day as the day of the Lord and don't bother others about how they relate with theirs. Mind your own business.

"Let no corrupt word proceed out of your mouth, but what is good for necessary edification, that it may impart grace to the hearers."
Ephesians 4:29 NKJV

God isn't just interested in what goes on in your heart, He is equally concerned about what comes out of your mouth. Words can heal or kill. Corrupt words are destructive while wholesome words are edifying.

God doesn't want you to speak corrupt (dirty, immoral, destructive) words because not only do they lack the grace to edify others, they also defile the speaker. So, whether you are serious or just playing, don't engage your mouth in corrupt words.

"Let your conduct be without covetousness; be content with such things as you have. For He Himself has said, "I will never leave you nor forsake you." So we may boldly say: "The LORD is my helper; I will not fear. What can man do to me?"

Hebrews 13:5-6 NKJV

A dictionary has defined covetousness as a strong wish to have something, especially something that belongs to someone else.

What is the cure for this? Be content and trust in the help of God for your needs. Already infected? Go for the cure.

"...let not the sun go down upon your wrath: Neither give place to the devil."
Ephesians 4:26-27 KJV

The Word of God says when you are angry, you shouldn't allow sunrise to become sunset with you still angry. Why? Because that will give a mighty foothold to the devil. He will hijack the anger and use it against you or anyone/anything precious to you.

Watch your anger level; it does more harm to you than your offender. Get it under control. The devil is eagerly waiting to take advantage of it if you allow him. Beware!!!

"...Let not your heart be troubled, neither let it be afraid."
John 14:27 KJV

A troubled heart is an anxious heart. A troubled heart is a depressed heart. A troubled heart is a confused heart. A troubled heart is a joyless heart. A troubled heart is a weak, weary heart, etc. *What can lead to these?* What you watch and hear in the news. What the people around you are saying. Dwelling on your weaknesses and flaws. Low self-esteem. Looking at your current unfavorable conditions, etc.

What can be done? DO NOT LET YOUR HEART BE TROUBLED. Don't allow it. Feed your heart with God's Word and do all it says regardless of the happenings around you. That's how to keep your heart from being troubled. Read Isaiah 26:3.

"Let us therefore...be thus minded..."
Philippians 3:15 KJV

What kind of mindset is the Lord drawing our attention to today? It's found in verses 13 and 14 of that same text: *'Brethren, I count not myself to have apprehended: but this one thing I do, forgetting those things which are behind, and reaching forth unto those things which are before, I press toward the mark for the prize of the high calling of God in Christ Jesus.'*

That's how Apostle Paul was able to fulfill his destiny in grand style. He never allowed anything in his past (great or not so great) to hold him back. He kept doing *ONLY ONE THING*: reaching out to the future and pursuing the fulfillment of God's purpose for his life. That's the mindset the Lord wants you to have as well. So, *let us...be thus minded...*

"Let him that stole steal no more..."
Ephesians 4:28 KJV

To steal is to take the property of another wrongfully and especially as a habitual or regular practice. Now, this could mean stealing from your parents, your partner, your employer, your associates, your group, your place of worship, etc.

And whether you are stealing their money, ideas, time, or anything else that is valuable to them, the Word of God expressly condemns it regardless of the method you employ - directly or indirectly. Thus saith the Lord: *'...steal no more...'*

"...Let your hands be strong..."
Zechariah 8:9 KJV

Weak hands hardly accomplish anything useful or glorious. Your ideas and concepts may be very fantastic, but weak-handed execution will frustrate the whole thing.

The Lord wants your hands to be strong so He can do great things through you - in your family, ministry, career, education, business, etc. So today, strengthen your hands as you get ready for divine adventure.

"...let it not be once named among you, as becometh saints..."
Ephesians 5:3-5 KJV

Becoming a child of God should affect all areas of our lives - our thoughts, speech, attitude, actions, disposition, relationships, choices, and our lifestyle in general.

As Christians, some things should never be mentioned concerning us. For example, our text says *"But fornication, and all uncleanness, or covetousness, let it not be once named among you, as becometh saints; Neither filthiness, nor foolish talking, nor jesting, which are not convenient: but rather giving of thanks. For this ye know, that no whoremonger, nor unclean person, nor covetous man, who is an idolater, hath any inheritance in the kingdom of Christ and of God."*

If we profess we are Christians, our lives should prove it. *Let (it) not be once named among you...*

"...let every man prove his own work, and then shall he have rejoicing in himself alone, and not in another. For every man shall bear his own burden."
Galatians 6:4-5 KJV

To 'prove' is to examine or test. God wants everyone to test their own work and be satisfied with the outcome. It's not enough to boast about what others have done, God wants you to be able to take pride in your own work too. That's when you can rejoice with some sense of fulfillment.

Why? *Every man shall bear his own burden.* If you do substandard jobs, for instance, you will bear the burden, which may imply you are never called for such jobs again.

If as a Minister of the Gospel you get an invitation to preach and you rush to the pulpit without adequate preparation and prayers, thereby delivering garbage instead of a message, you will bear the burden of losing the opportunity to be invited again. The list goes on and on. Consider what you do and how you do it. Would you be pleased if others did yours that way?

"...let your children tell their children, and their children another generation".
Joel 1:3 KJV

God doesn't want any generation to be ignorant of His knowledge, power, and manifestations. And that's why He has charged parents (biological and spiritual) to tell their children about Him and the children to also tell their own children and on and on.

'Pass it on' is the name of the game. For example, in 2 Timothy 1:5 KJV, Lois (grandmother) passed it on to Eunice (mother) and she, in turn, passed it on to Timothy (son). That's your responsibility as a parent (in whatever capacity).

"...let us, who are of the day, be sober..."
1 Thessalonians 5:8 KJV

The life we have been called to live in Christ requires being sober and vigilant. We are not to live carelessly all in the name of faith.

People of faith are not careless or reckless people. You don't act carelessly while you keep confessing that your faith will sustain you. You may end up not liking the results. You are to be sober and careful with your thoughts, words, actions, etc. We are of the day, let us live as those who have light.

"Let us draw near with a true heart in full assurance of faith..."
Hebrews 10:22 KJV

When approaching God in the place of prayer, our attitude must depict humility and sincerity. To draw near with a true heart implies not having any falsehood in your heart. It also implies coming to God with an open heart to receive from Him and not forcing what you have already decided on Him.

God hates deception. Don't approach the throne of grace with any form of falsehood in your heart. God knows who is pretending and who is not.

"...let him ask of God, that giveth to all men liberally, and upbraideth not; and it shall be given him."

James 1:5 KJV

That verse started by saying *"If any of you lack wisdom..."* Now, it says *let him ask of God*. We fail to receive many times because we don't ask of God. We complain to God, we murmur about it in His Presence, we feel unhappy about it from day to day but what the Bible says is *'let him ask of God'*. You've got to ask to receive (Matthew 7:7-8).

What can you ask of God? Anything you lack (wisdom, power, strength, relationship, money, family, help, health, grace, etc). *If any man LACK...let him ask of God Who giveth generously and doesn't rebuke people for asking.*

"Let us go forth therefore unto him without the camp, bearing his reproach."

Hebrews 13:13 KJV

Jesus Christ wasn't crucified in a Temple; He was brutally crucified naked on a hill in public view - with different people watching from near and afar. There was nothing confidential or private about His shameful death on the Cross (Hebrews 12:2).

Now, if Jesus passed through all that public shame to redeem you and I from perishing in our sins, is it too much to also identify with Him publicly - regardless of the reproach, ridicule, or persecution we face in the process?

We discuss sports publicly, we discuss the weather publicly, we talk to both friends and strangers about celebrities, politics, the economy, etc. But when it comes to talking about Jesus publicly, we feel embarrassed. We don't want anyone to know we belong to Him.

Friends, Jesus wants you to make Him known PUBLICLY. He doesn't want to be kept within the four walls of your church. He wants to be revealed in malls, markets, offices, social media, on trains, airplanes, etc. That's why He died publicly.

LET US GO FORTH UNTO HIM OUTSIDE THE CAMP BEARING HIS REPROACH. That's where He wants to be made known.

"Let brotherly love continue."
Hebrews 13:1 KJV

Brotherly love. That's the kind of love the early disciples exhibited - Read Acts 4:32-37. Things are however different these days. We now want people to earn our love by the things they do for us. We give gifts in return for gifts received. If someone doesn't honor our invitation to an event, we ensure we don't honor theirs as well.

We only give when there is a chance of getting something back - transactional love. Brotherly love isn't like that; it keeps loving and keeps giving even when the recipient doesn't deserve it or give anything in return. And that's what the Bible says should continue. How is your love life?

"Let no man say when he is tempted, I am tempted of God: for God cannot be tempted with evil, neither tempteth he any man: But every man is tempted, when he is drawn

away of his own lust, and enticed. Then when lust hath conceived, it bringeth forth sin: and sin, when it is finished, bringeth forth death."
James 1:13-15 KJV

Be not deceived, God tempts no one. According to a dictionary, to tempt is to entice or attempt to entice (someone) to do or acquire something that they find attractive but know to be wrong or not beneficial.

Your temptations most times originate from your lusts (uncontrolled desires). No man can fall into adultery if he hasn't been secretly desiring other women aside from his wife. In the same way, no one is likely to steal if the strong desire to have what others have hasn't been first nursed in their hearts.

Your lustful desires are magnetic; they attract all manners of temptations into your life - thereby bringing along sin and eventual death. What is it that you repeatedly lust after? Be careful; most of your temptations will come from there.

"...let every man be swift to hear, slow to speak, slow to wrath: For the wrath of man worketh not the righteousness of God."
James 1:19-20 KJV

The Lord wants every one of us to be quick to listen but slow to respond and slow to get angry. It has been said that a lot of us listen to respond instead of listening to understand. While listening, we are busy rehearsing our next response. We don't learn or gain wisdom that way.

Someone has said we are given two ears and one mouth for a reason; we are expected to listen at least twice before we respond once. It also says *'slow to wrath'* because man's anger NEVER accomplishes God's righteousness.

How well are you obeying this scriptural injunction? Are you a listener or all you do is talk and get angry? Do some self-assessment and adjust as necessary.

"...let none of you suffer as a murderer, or as a thief, or as an evildoer, or as a busybody in other men's matters. Yet if any man suffer as a Christian, let him not be ashamed; but let him glorify God on this behalf."
1 Peter 4:15–16 KJV

Certain sufferings characterize Christianity, but there are great eternal rewards for every one of them we endure.

However, our text says we shouldn't suffer as evildoers. That is, as Christians, we are not supposed to suffer because of our wrongdoing. If any Christian suffers because of the wrong things they have done, there is no reward for that.

The sufferings that attract divine rewards include persecution for Christ's sake, not taking revenge when assaulted, false accusations, mockery for the sake of Christ, parents' withdrawal of support from their children just because they decided for Jesus, etc.

If you are being maltreated or reproached because of your connection with Jesus, rejoice; great is your reward with the Father. Just hold on and stay positive.

"...let him pray...."
James 5:13 KJV

The Word of God says *'Is any among you afflicted? let him pray...'* The simplest definition of affliction according to a dictionary is something that causes pain or suffering.

So, is anything or anyone causing you pain or suffering? The Lord doesn't want you to cry, curse, complain, lament, worry, grumble, murmur, or go into depression.

Rather, the Lord wants you to pray. That's the response He expects when you are afflicted. That's how He intends to put an end to your affliction. *'Is any among you afflicted? let him pray...'*

Note also that He didn't say *'let them pray for him'*. It is you who will do the praying. That's how your affliction will end. So, with this knowledge, what are you going to do with that situation or person that has been causing you pain or suffering?

"...let him sing...."
James 5:13 KJV

The Word of God says *'Is any merry? let him sing psalms.'* The simplest definition of merry according to a dictionary is cheerful (lively). And Psalms imply sacred songs or hymns.

So, are you cheerful or happy about some particular news? Or have you received something you have been praying about for a long time? Whatever it is that causes you to be glad and lively, the Lord doesn't want you to hide or suppress it. You know, some people don't want others to know they are happy. They prefer to be pitied than to be celebrated.

Well, the Lord wants you to SING. That's the response He expects when you are cheerful. That's how He wants to be appreciated. *'Is any among you merry? let him sing psalms.'*

Note also that He said to sing sacred songs or hymns (psalms). So, you don't sing songs that dishonor God. The songs have to glorify Him - sacred.

With this knowledge, how are you going to respond to that development or person that has brought gladness to your heart?

"...let him call for the elders of the church; and let them pray over him...."
James 5:14 KJV

The Word of God says *'Is any sick among you? let him call for the elders of the church; and let them pray over him, anointing him with oil in the name of the Lord: And the prayer of faith shall save the sick, and the Lord shall raise him up; and if he have committed sins, they shall be forgiven him.'*

That's the approach God expects if sickness happens to be your own battle. He wants you to send for the elders of the church so they can pray for you. Now, He didn't say call for the elders of your village or community; rather He said the elders of the church. So, those elders must be in right standing with the Lord - the Head of the Church.

Also, elders don't necessarily mean the old people in your church. Anyone who knows more than you in the things of God qualifies as your elder in faith - whether they are bishops or not. Send for such people and as they do what our text says in faith, the Lord will honor their prayers and raise you up. So, are you sick? Go ahead and do what James 5:14 says, and all shall be well.

"...Let him know, that he which converteth the sinner from the error of his way shall save a soul from death, and shall hide a multitude of sins."
James 5:19-20 KJV

The Word of God says *"Brethren, if any of you do err from the truth, and one convert him; Let him know, that he which converteth the sinner from the error of his way shall save a soul from death, and shall hide a multitude of sins."*

When you see someone erring from the truth and you intervene towards getting them back to the truth, you are practically saving a soul from death. Think about that!

Who can you turn from errors today? Whose soul are you going to save from death this season?

"...let him ask in faith, nothing wavering. For he that wavereth is like a wave of the sea driven with the wind and tossed."
James 1:6 KJV

God is a Spirit, and He lives in the Spirit realm. So, all your requests or prayers can only be heard and responded to in the Spirit. In fact, all you want God to do for you will take place first in the Spirit before they ever show up in the physical.

With this understanding, you need to live by faith; because only faith can connect you to the activities going on in the realm of the Spirit.

You don't just ask and begin to doubt or waver all because you can't see anything in the physical yet. That's why the Word of God says *'...let him ask in faith...'*

How have you been asking?

"...let him hear what the Spirit saith unto the churches..."
Revelation 2:7 KJV

Thus saith the Lord: *'He that hath an ear, let him hear what the Spirit saith unto the churches...'* Daily, you will be faced with the decision to either follow your natural (carnal) inclinations or spiritual (godly) promptings.

The Spirit of the Lord is not silent about the issues in your life. He wants to guide you so you don't fall into errors. It will be in your own interest to yield to His guidance instead of giving your flesh an upper hand.

Where is the starting point? The Word of God - Your Bible. Allowing the Word of God to govern your life daily is equivalent to hearing what the Spirit says to the churches. Today, will you hear?

"Let that therefore abide in you, which ye have heard from the beginning. If that which ye have heard from the beginning shall remain in you, ye also shall continue in the Son, and in the Father."
1 John 2:24 KJV

Nothing breeds backsliding like allowing what was delivered into your hands from the very beginning to slip off your hands.

Some were good Christians until they started questioning the Christlike virtues in their lives. These virtues had been in their lives for years because they were willing to receive them and live by them. But all of a sudden, they now see these virtues as *'old school'* and outdated.

To CONTINUE with Jesus doesn't necessarily require fresh revelations; all it takes is to let His Words which you received from the very beginning ABIDE in you. Don't allow modern-day doctrines to destroy your Christlike foundation.

"...let patience have her perfect work, that ye may be perfect and entire, wanting nothing."

James 1:4 KJV

The Word of God makes it clear that faith must be combined with patience to experience the fulfillment of God's promises in our lives - Hebrews 6:12, Hebrews 10:36.

Now, patience is not a gift; so, it doesn't answer to anointing oil or laying of hands. Rather, it is a fruit to be borne - Galatians 5:22. God consciously brings certain situations and people our way to teach us patience, and it is our responsibility to allow our patience to grow so we don't miss out on God's best for us.

Let patience have her perfect work in you; that's how to receive God's very best.

"...let us walk by the same rule..."
Philippians 3:16 KJV

Jesus Christ walked this same planet thousands of years ago and He's now in glory. Now, while He was here, He lived by certain rules. For instance, He loved others, forgave, rebuked hypocrisy, showed compassion, prayed, fasted, gave to the poor, obeyed authorities and He never allowed His personal feelings to prevent Him from doing the will of the Father. He did all that by the power of the Holy Spirit at work in Him- Acts 10:38.

This is our time and that same Holy Spirit has been given to us. *Let us walk by the same rule* so we too can end up where Jesus ended up - ETERNAL GLORY.

"...let not that man think that he shall receive any thing of the Lord. A double minded man is unstable in all his ways."
James 1:7-8 KJV

The ONLY WAY to relate with GOD is through faith - Hebrews 11:6. And the MAIN ENEMY of this way is DOUBT. Now, a dictionary has described *'doubt'* as a feeling of uncertainty or lack of conviction.

No matter how spiritual you may appear to be, and regardless of your church titles, once you allow doubt (lack of conviction) to attack your faith in God, you will become unstable in all your ways and you will not be able to receive ANYTHING from the Lord. Do not DOUBT GOD FOR ANY REASON!

"Let the brother of low degree rejoice in that he is exalted"
James 1:9 KJV

Are you a Christian with humble circumstances? Do people look down on you because you are not as rich and famous as others in society? Rejoice; you mean so much to God, and He highly regards you. The Amplified Bible puts it this way - *'Let the brother in humble circumstances glory in his high position [as a born-again believer, called to the true riches and to be an heir of God];'.*

God highly treasures you and all His wealth is at your disposal - the true riches. Don't compromise your faith in God through cheating, bribery, or other evil things people do to get by in life. You are more than that. You are so special to God, and it is high time you started seeing yourself like that.

"Let no man therefore judge you..."
Colossians 2:16 KJV

If you are a child of God and you live according to the teachings of Jesus as well as the principles of God's Word, you are at peace with God. Your first responsibility in everything you say and do is to please God; not man.

Don't be afraid of what people will say when you know you are in God's will. No one on earth has the moral right to judge you when God hasn't judged you. Don't let the fear of man's judgment or opinions set you against your God. Proverbs 29:25 KJV says *'The fear of man bringeth a snare: but whoso putteth his trust in the LORD shall be safe.'* Live to primarily please God; He's the only One described as the *'Righteous Judge'*. No one else.

"...let him speak as the oracles of God..."
1 Peter 4:10-11 KJV

The Word of God says: *'As every man hath received the gift, even so minister the same one to another, as good stewards of the manifold grace of God. If any man speak, let him speak as the oracles of God; if any man minister, let him do it as of the ability which God giveth: that God in all things may be glorified through Jesus Christ, to whom be praise and dominion for ever and ever. Amen.'*

Friends, God's Word does not need man's help. The Word of God is POTENT enough to generate any result God desires to generate with it. All Mary received was a Word, and her virginity couldn't stop her from becoming pregnant with Jesus.

And Peter? All He received was a Word (COME), and water became solid ground under his feet. He practically walked on water. Say whatever God puts in your heart to say and do only what He asks you to do with the ability He supplies. There is no need for gymnastics or decorations. He will do the rest without your help.

"Let not then your good be evil spoken of"
Romans 14:16 KJV

As God's children, we have been called to do good works everywhere we find ourselves. That's our nature and that's what God expects from us every time. However, because the Word of God says *'wisdom is profitable to direct'* we are expected to carry out our good works with wisdom.

For instance, there is nothing wrong with counseling a member of the opposite gender who needs help. But when you begin to develop some unhealthy intimacy with them to the extent that the counseling now takes place in dark rooms (behind closed doors) with just the two of you, you are beginning to give opportunities for your good to be evil spoken of.

Don't allow your good to be evil spoken of. Maintain a clear conscience not only with yourself but also with others. Give no room for suspicion and don't attract blasphemous words to your Heavenly Father by the way you live. Take heed!

"Let the elders that rule well be counted worthy of double honour, especially they who labor in the word and doctrine."
1 Timothy 5:17 KJV

In the Body of Christ, God has ordained that those who are mature in spiritual things and hold ecclesiastical positions (the elders) should be treated with double honor, especially those who labor to make the Word of God available to others.

None of such people deserves to be neglected, ignored, or insulted. The Lord will not take it lightly. God holds them in high esteem and so should you. Learn to appreciate and honor your spiritual leaders. God demands that.

"...let him that is athirst come. And whosoever will, let him take the water of life freely."
Revelation 22:17 KJV

Jesus said He didn't come for the righteous (those who feel they are doing okay as far as keeping God's commandments is concerned). Rather, He came for those who are tired of their burdens of sin, those who desire a change of story, those who know there is more to being in relationship with God than merely keeping the Ten Commandments, those who are not just playing church but are hungry and thirsty for divine encounters.

That's why He said *'let him that is athirst come and take the water of life freely.'* Are you a genuine seeker? Jesus wants to meet you. Speak to Him in prayer today.

"Let us be glad and rejoice..."
Revelation 19:7 KJV

Even though most of the situations around us suggest otherwise, the Lord still expects us to *be glad and rejoice*. You may look at everything happening around the world, things happening in your own life, and the kind of news headlines we see these days and ask yourself - what's there to rejoice about?

Well, you can rejoice about being still alive. After all, *a living dog is better than a dead lion*, saith the scriptures. And one other reason to rejoice is all the beautiful plans God still has for you

(Jeremiah 29:11). Romans 12:12 says *'Rejoicing in hope...'* You can rejoice in hope. That's celebrating your testimonies in advance even before they arrive. This kind of rejoicing will get your testimonies delivered unhindered. No matter what, DO NOT LOSE YOUR JOY!

"...let it die..."
Zechariah 11:9 KJV

When it comes to walking with God the way He has ordained, it is very important to know that living is practically impossible until dying has taken place.

As a matter of fact, death is what gives birth to life as far as God is concerned. Jesus said if you try to gain your life, you will lose it; but if you choose to lose it, then you will gain it.

In Galatians 2:20, Apostle Paul said he was crucified with Christ, that the life he had wasn't his anymore but that which the Lord birthed in him (after he gave up his).

Let it die... What? Your Adamic (carnal) nature. Your flesh. That's the only way to experience the life of Christ in fullness.

"...let God be true, but every man a liar..."
Romans 3:4 KJV

Numbers 23:19 says *God is not a man that He should lie.* Every word that proceeds from the Lord is true. If at any point in time you listen to a message or hear something contrary to the Word of God, you have a responsibility to treat such as a lie. God doesn't change His standards. He said *'I am the Lord, I change not.'*

Watch what you hear and what you watch; only treat them as truth as long as they are in line with God's Word. Once they go against the Word, *let God be true, but every man a liar.*

"...let every man have his own wife, and let every woman have her own husband."
1 Corinthians 7:2 KJV

The foundation of the Lord concerning marriage stands sure. There is nothing unclear about it. The Word of God says *'Nevertheless, to avoid fornication, let every man have his own wife, and let every woman have her own husband.'*

Notice it didn't say *'let every man have a girlfriend, hot babe, sex partner or side chick'*. Rather, it says *'let every man have HIS OWN WIFE'* - not wives, another person's wife, or another man (same-sex union).

Also, for the woman, she's to have HER OWN HUSBAND - *not husbands, a boyfriend, sex partner, or another woman* (same-sex union).

Be not deceived; no level of civilization or movement can change God's standard. Psalm 119:89 says *'Forever O Lord, thy word is settled in heaven.'* If it is not done according to the Word, it is still FORNICATION. And no fornicator shall inherit the Kingdom of God (Galatians 5:19-21). Be warned!

"...let the wives be (subject) to their own husbands in every thing."
Ephesians 5:24 KJV

The Word of God says *'Therefore as the church is subject unto Christ, so let the wives be to their own husbands in every thing.'* The church is subject to Christ in everything. We take instructions from Jesus, we honor Jesus, we submit ourselves to follow His will even when it's not easy to do so, we don't argue with Christ and we don't claim individuality when it comes to our relationship with Him. In all, we regard Jesus to be our Head and we relate with Him accordingly.

Now, that's the expectation of God concerning every Christian wife concerning their husbands. Marriage only works when the parties involved choose to maintain the divine order. Sister, how is your marriage?

"...let every one of you in particular so love his wife even as himself..."
Ephesians 5:33 KJV

Ephesians 5:25 KJV says *'Husbands, love your wives, even as Christ also loved the church, and gave himself for it'*. Christ doesn't cheat on the church, He doesn't force the church to do anything, He constantly thinks about the church and always does what is best for the church, He cherishes and nourishes the church, He ensures the church feels safe with Him, and of course, He doesn't beat the church.

God expects Christian husbands to love their wives this way - just as Jesus loves the church sacrificially. Failure to do this may result in Christian husbands experiencing hindered prayers - 1 Peter 3:7. Marriage only works when the parties involved decide to maintain the divine order. Brother, how is your marriage?

"...let us not fight against God."
Acts 23:9 KJV

There is one type of battle no mortal can win; it's the battle against God. The fact that some don't believe in God's existence doesn't stop Him from being God; neither does it mean He won't demonstrate His omnipotence when necessary.

To know the will of God and go against it can be regarded as fighting against God. Also, to make attempts to stop or prevent what God is doing in an individual's life, community or nation simply implies fighting against God.

Stop fighting a battle you can never win. Submit to God and join the winning party. That's how to escape a life of defeat.

"...let your peace come upon it: but if it be not worthy, let your peace return to you."
Matthew 10:13 KJV

The Gospel of Jesus Christ is a message of Peace because He is the *Prince of Peace* (Isaiah 9:6). The Lord wants His followers to offer His invitation to salvation to others peacefully, as written in our text above.

There is no such thing as a forceful approach in evangelism. Jesus only wants to be introduced, not defended or forced on others. He said *'let him that is thirsty come...'*

Following Jesus MUST BE A CONSCIOUS DECISION; not a coerced endeavor. Both the presentation and the acceptance of the Gospel of Jesus Christ must be done PEACEFULLY!

"...Let us go into the next towns, that I may preach there also: for therefore came I forth."

Mark 1:38 KJV

That statement in our text was made by our Lord Jesus Christ; and as Christians, we are called to follow in His footsteps. Jesus didn't localize the gospel. That is, He didn't restrict the message of salvation to a particular place. He had a broad perspective regarding sinners' conversion.

As Ministers of the gospel and as Christians generally, we are not only called to minister to those within the four walls of our church buildings. Jesus' mandate for us is *'to seek and to save.'* The Lord wants us to go to other locations to declare His saving grace. He wants us to leave our *'99 sheep'* behind and go look for the missing *'1'*. And that's a clear call into missions.

You can reach out to other locations by GOING (personally), SENDING (sponsoring missions and sending out missionaries), OR PRAYING (wetting the ground for harvest and upholding the work of missions in those locations). One way or the other, JUST GET INVOLVED. It's a Mandate!

"...let it not be that outward adorning of plaiting the hair, and of wearing of gold, or of putting on of apparel; But let it be the hidden man of the heart, in that which is not corruptible, even the ornament of a meek and quiet spirit, which is in the sight of God of great price."
1 Peter 3:3-4 KJV

It's okay to be mindful of our appearances. Wearing nice clothes, using beautiful pieces of jewelry, doing makeovers as well as engaging hairstylists' expertise are not bad in themselves. The only challenge is when they begin to attract more time and devotion from us than we make available to develop our spiritual lives - in meekness and quiet spirit.

Read our text again. One is of great price in the sight of God while the other is not. Which one do you think should get your undivided attention? Think about it!

"...let him refrain his tongue..."
1 Peter 3:10 KJV

Who should refrain his tongue? Everybody? No. Who then? Look at 1 Peter 3:10-11 KJV: *'For he that will love life, and see good days, let him refrain his tongue from evil, and his lips that they speak no guile: Let him eschew evil, and do good; let him seek peace, and ensue it.'*

There it is. The fellow who loves to be alive and see good days is the one who should refrain his tongue from evil and deception. He's also expected to do good, seek peace and depart from anything evil. To not fulfill these responsibilities is to hate being alive, and it's also a sure way to see bad days. What then? Make a choice!

"...let us go on unto perfection..."
Hebrews 6:1-2 KJV

The Word of God says: *'Therefore leaving the principles of the doctrine of Christ, let us go on unto perfection; not laying again the foundation of repentance from dead works, and of faith toward God, Of the doctrine of baptisms, and of laying on of hands, and of resurrection of the dead, and of eternal judgment.'*

If as a Christian of many years, you still need somebody following you up before you read your Bible or you still need to be taught afresh what it means to repent from dead works and to have faith toward God among other elementary doctrines of Christ, YOU ARE NOT GROWING.

Your situation can be compared to an adult running around in baby diapers and crying every time they need food. That's what it looks like to God.

Let us go on unto perfection..., Let us grow in grace and in the knowledge of God, Let us stop arguing about the types of baptism and other elementary principles, Let us grow up and become mature in the things of God - that's when we can really be useful in the things of God.

"Let as many servants as are under the yoke count their own masters worthy of all honour, that the name of God and his doctrine be not blasphemed. And they that have believing masters, let them not despise them, because they are brethren; but rather do them service, because they are faithful and beloved, partakers of the benefit. These things teach and exhort."
1 Timothy 6:1-2 KJV

What exactly is the Lord saying in this text? Servants (employees) should render faithful services to their Masters (employers), honoring them so that God's Name will not be blasphemed. And if those Masters are believers, servants should see and treat them as brethren. The Lord wants these things to be taught to you, and we just did.

"...let us prophesy according to the proportion of faith;"
Romans 12:6 KJV

The Word of God says *'Having then gifts differing according to the grace that is given to us, whether prophecy, let us prophesy according to the proportion of faith;'*

No man can operate beyond the level of grace God makes available to him; so, it's a futile exercise to even try. Prophesying shouldn't be a function of *'my members are expecting to hear me prophesy'*; and it shouldn't be geared towards making some dishonest gain from unsuspecting people.

Just because someone very rich and influential comes to your church on a particular Sunday doesn't mean they have to be impressed with a prophecy so they could make large donations to your church. If you must prophesy, *prophesy according to the proportion of faith*, based on the grace of God available to you in that area. That's how God gets glorified and you don't get whipped, but blessed.

"...let us consider one another in order to stir up love and good works,"
Hebrews 10:24 NKJV

Friends, there is no better way to gauge our level of love than by observing how we treat others. In Christianity, we are not called to be self-centered. Rather, we are called and commanded to love others.

According to our text, to consider others implies saying and doing what benefits others and not just what we feel is good for us only. When we begin to consider what's good for others before we make our decisions, take steps, or even speak, we will soon discover what it really means to love others, and people will respond (be stirred up) in love as well. May the grace to consider others in love come upon us all this season in Jesus' Name.

"Let us labour therefore to enter into that rest, lest any man fall after the same example of unbelief."
Hebrews 4:11 KJV

According to verses 9 and 10 of Hebrews 4, there is a rest the Lord has ordained for His people; when all work will cease. It is not just sabbath rest, neither is it a vacation. It is God's kind of rest.

Only those who belong and stay true to Jesus will enjoy this rest. Those who live in unbelief cannot enjoy it. It is a FAITH REST.

The Lord is therefore encouraging us according to the text above to labor to enter that rest. He doesn't want any of us to miss it through unbelief. So, start fighting your doubts as well as your carnal inclinations; and learn to trust in the Lord. That's how to enter into God's rest. You will not miss it in Jesus' Name.

"...let us have grace, whereby we may serve God acceptably..."
Hebrews 12:28 KJV

Serving God is not a function of how knowledgeable or strong you are; rather it is a function of the grace made available to you.

Whatsoever you want to do for God, go ahead and ask Him for the grace to do it. Christianity is all about grace. Living the Christian life is to be set apart from evil and be set apart unto God.

Don't try to serve God with mere human strength (struggles); rather have grace and let the Ancient of Days bear you up in His Everlasting Arms.

Grace is what makes your sweat invisible, yet your results undeniable. Ask for more grace for greater impact in Jesus' Name.

"Let thy garments be always white..."
Ecclesiastes 9:8 KJV

When you came to the knowledge of the saving grace of Jesus Christ and gladly accepted His offer of salvation, you were given a garment in the spirit - the robe of righteousness. It's a white robe indicating the nature of God in you- Isaiah 61:10, Revelation 19:8.

Now it's up to you to keep your garment clean - always white, by the help of the Holy Ghost. Stay away from sin (defilement) and work out your own salvation with fear and trembling. Don't allow your garment to be stained for any reason. Those with stained garments shall end up on the wrong side of eternity. That will not be your portion in Jesus' Name.

"...let thy words be few."
Ecclesiastes 5:2 KJV

Why does the Lord want us to practice this verse - *let thy words be few?* Well, it could be because the power of death and life lies in the tongue. Words can kill and words can heal. Words can destroy and words can build.

Also, it could be because He knows that when we are busy talking, we are not listening. He wants us to be swift (quick) to listen but slow to speak. And most importantly, it could be because of Proverbs 10:19 KJV which says *'In the multitude of words there wanteth not sin: but he that refraineth his lips is wise.'*

To talk too much leads to sin, and sin is what causes spiritual death. You sure don't want that; do you? So, *let thy words be few.*

"...let not thine heart be hasty to utter any thing before God: for God is in heaven, and thou upon earth..."

Ecclesiastes 5:2 KJV

The Word of God admonishes us to do more listening than speaking when in God's Presence. *Let not thine heart be hasty to utter anything before God...* Those who rush to make impulsive vows that they cannot keep before God out of emotions are not practicing this verse of the Bible. God prefers you not to vow at all than to vow or promise Him something and not keep it.

When in God's Presence (in church or at home), *let not your heart be hasty*. Don't ensnare yourself with your own words. Be wise!

"...let us go up to the mountain of the LORD, to the house of the God of Jacob; and he will teach us of his ways, and we will walk in his paths..."

Isaiah 2:3 KJV

Before Samson ended up on Delilah's lap - where his destiny got short-circuited - he had the habit of always going down (Judges 14:1,5,7,19; 15:8 KJV).

You can't live an *'up'* life when all you do is go down. You can't afford to go down in your prayer life, giving, praises, evangelism, Bible study, and preparation for your eternal home. You may end up in the camp of your enemies like Samson did if you keep going down (Judges 16:21). To prevent this, make going up a lifestyle. Don't remain in your current spiritual level; go up in your knowledge of God and go up in your fellowship with Him. That's how to escape the *'down'* life. Tell yourself: *'I will go up.'*

"...let us reason together, saith the LORD: though your sins be as scarlet, they shall be as white as snow; though they be red like crimson, they shall be as wool.

Isaiah 1:18 KJV

God is a very persistent Lover; He doesn't give up on His people easily. Look at His invitation in our text above; He's reaching out to His children (His chosen people) who have wandered away. He's like saying *'Come on, let's talk about it. I can take care of your sins if you will let me. You shouldn't remain in your dirt; I can cleanse you.'*

Now, for God to have extended this invitation means He's still in love. Accept the invitation today and get out of your sinful state. Let the Lord wash you with the Precious Blood of His Son, Jesus Christ. You can be cleansed again. Will you respond today?

"Let every thing that hath breath praise the LORD..."
Psalm 150:6 KJV

So, your day didn't go as planned? Yeah, I understand. But if you are still breathing, you've got to praise the Lord. Your expectation didn't come to pass? Yeah, that can be painful. But are you still breathing? If yes, you will still have to praise the Lord.

You are critically ill? Oh, am so sorry. That's not fun at all, and I can only pray that the Lord will lay His healing Hand upon you. But in the meantime, if you can still breathe, God expects your praises. No matter who you are, where you are, or what you do, if you still have breath, you must praise the Lord.

"...let us worship and bow down: let us kneel before the LORD our maker. For he is our God; and we are the people of his pasture, and the sheep of his hand."
Psalm 95:6-7 KJV

Worship isn't about us at all. It's all about the One Who alone deserves it - the Almighty God. Bowing down as well as kneeling before the LORD our Maker implies total humility and absolute submission to His Omnipotence and Sovereignty. We are just sheep of His pasture. He can do without us, but we CANNOT do without Him - John 15:5.

So, next time when you worship, remember the One you are worshiping deserves all your humility and submission. He owes you nothing; you owe Him your very life. Start worshiping with understanding.

"Let them give glory unto the LORD..."
Isaiah 42:12 KJV

Whatever you can boast of today didn't come because of your smartness, intelligence, connection, or mental prowess. Be it your academic success, marital bliss, prosperous business, or successful ministry, God made them possible.

God is the Giver of good things, and you are just a privileged beneficiary of His magnanimous goodness. Therefore, LEARN to give God the glory for your results in life. Some are smarter than you, yet they have nothing to show for it. The difference is simply God's mercy.

"...let your ear receive the word of his mouth..."
Jeremiah 9:20 KJV

God has been speaking since the beginning of creation, and He still speaks. The challenge however is *'how many people are willing to receive or accept what He says?'*

You see, most times God's Word doesn't align with our thinking or mindset; and as such, we simply refuse to accept it. But if you read Isaiah 55:8-9, you will understand why His Word hardly makes sense to any man. His thinking is TOTALLY different from ours. So, what are you expected to do now? *Tell your ear to receive the word of His mouth.* You must hear and accept the Word of God as the final authority over your life and situations by CONSCIOUS DECISION, even when it makes no sense at all. That's the right attitude to possess if you must keep hearing from God.

"Let another man praise thee, and not thine own mouth; a stranger, and not thine own lips."
Proverbs 27:2 KJV

'If not for me, that project would have ended in a complete mess.'
'If I had not intervened when their parents died, those children wouldn't have been able to go to school.'
'If not for my timely input, my Church wouldn't have been able to hold that program.'

These statements and similar ones may be very true, but they aren't supposed to be heard from your mouth. The Word of God is against self-praise: it's seen as an unhealthy form of boasting. According to our text, your accolades and applause should come from others; not yourself. That's one way to learn how to remain humble regardless of your achievements.

"...let us stand together..."
Isaiah 50:8 KJV

There is a popular saying: *'united we stand, divided we fall.'* And this is very correct. When we stand together as the Body of Christ, for instance, the devil and his agents will find it so difficult to infiltrate and destroy us from within. But when all we post on social media is about how one brother or sister in the church fought with their Pastor, and how somebody refused to greet us, the devil won't find it so hard to deal with us from within.

Let us stand together as brothers and sisters. Let us pray for one another when we notice any faults or shortcomings. That's God's expectation from His children. Jesus prayed for us - His followers - in John 21 that we will be one just as He is one with the Father. *Let us stand together;* that's the only way to be all God wants us to be as a Church.

"...let them take counsel together..."
Isaiah 45:21 KJV

Are people ganging up against you in your place of work, school, family, or even church just because you decided to live for Jesus and glorify Him with your life? Relax! Don't fret. They are all allowed to take counsel together against you; but as long as it is not of the Lord, it shall come to naught.

Isaiah 8:10 affirms this: *'Take counsel together, and it shall come to nought; speak the word, and it shall not stand: for God is with us.'* This will always be your testimony as long as you are on the Lord's side. Don't fight back; just rest in the Lord. They will never succeed against you.

"...let us walk in the light of the LORD..."
Isaiah 2:5 KJV

Why is it so important that as God's children we walk in the light of the LORD? Look at Isaiah 60:2; it says *'...behold, the darkness shall cover the earth, and gross darkness the people...'*

This world's system is subject to darkness, and only those who choose to walk in the light can make any meaningful headway in it. If you follow the system or ways of this world, you will end up confused and empty because darkness implies a lack of vision.

Walk in the light of the Lord; let His Spirit and His Word guide your affairs. Don't do life like everyone else; approach life with a sense of divine purpose and you will end up fulfilled, the devil notwithstanding.

"...let us be silent there..."
Jeremiah 8:14 KJV

According to Ecclesiastes 3:7, there's a time to keep silent, and a time to speak. Silence can be a very great virtue if properly channeled or engaged. As a matter of fact, the Word of God encourages us to be swift to listen but slow to speak.

Where should you be silent then? When you are in God's Presence, don't just speak; also listen through silence. You will be able to receive into your spirit whatever He may be saying to you.

Also, when you are around those who are deep in wisdom, learn from them through silence. What you want to say you already know; but what they want to say, you don't know yet... Just some pieces of advice there.

"...let them return unto thee..."
Jeremiah 15:19 KJV

I wish to announce to you straight away that this life isn't a bed of roses; not even for the most spiritual among men. Jesus said *'in this world you shall have tribulations'* - that's the way this imperfect world is configured to run.

However, as God's children, our attitude should be positive. We don't want to handle things the way the unbelievers do. We should not be consuming alcohol, smoking cigarettes and weed, engaging in prostitution or any other kind of immorality, using drugs, gambling, among other ungodly activities - all in the name of trying to suppress the effects of our problems.

Challenges of life shouldn't push you away from your God; rather, they should draw you closer to Him. Why? He's the ONLY WAY out of all your predicaments. So, if you have left God because of your problems; return to Him TODAY. He still cares about you.

"Let thy fountain be blessed: and rejoice with the wife of thy youth. Let her be as the loving hind and pleasant roe; let her breasts satisfy thee at all times; and be thou ravished always with her love. And why wilt thou, my son, be ravished with a strange woman, and embrace the bosom of a stranger?"
Proverbs 5:18-20 KJV

The above scripture is located in the Book of Wisdom: Proverbs. That is, what you just read in those verses are words of wisdom. And not following them simply implies embracing folly.

Your spouse may not be perfect; she may have many flaws which you didn't discover before you married her. But the Word of God says *'LET HER BE...'* That's the key.

She may not *be as the loving hind or pleasant roe,* but you can *'let her be as the loving hind or pleasant roe'.* You can *'let her breasts satisfy you at ALL TIMES (before and even after giving birth and breastfeeding your children)'.* You can *'let her love fill your heart always'* regardless of her nagging nature. How? Through decision.

You MUST decide to love. Agape love has nothing to do with feeling but CHOICE. Whenever you see *'let'* in the Bible, it means you can do it and God expects you to do it - because it's within your power. Start loving your spouse by DECISION!

"...let the oppressed go free, and...break every yoke..."
Isaiah 58:6 KJV

God is very much against bondage. This is especially so because He is the Author of liberty. 2 Corinthians 3:17 says *'...where the Spirit of the Lord is, there is liberty.'*

He wants us to be instruments of liberation to the oppressed. He wants us to speak up for those who can't speak for themselves; He wants us to orchestrate the deliverance of the downtrodden and He surely wants us to do everything within our power to ensure His people enjoy the freedom He gives.

So, if you can, use legal means to set people free; use financial means to set people free; use your influence or social status to set people free; use your political power to set people free; and if you don't have any of those, go on your knees and pray for the freedom of those who are oppressed.

One way or the other, join God in this business of letting the oppressed go free, and your reward shall be great in Jesus' Name.

"...let him be your fear, and let him be your dread."
Isaiah 8:13 KJV

The Word of God says: *'Sanctify the LORD of hosts himself; and let him be your fear, and let him be your dread.'* The fear of man is a snare. The Lord does not want us to be afraid of what men can do to us. We can't afford to offend God just because we want to please men.

In all your dealings in life, learn to fear God. Only God can destroy a man both on earth and in eternity. And only Him can save both here and in eternity. Fear God!

"...let him do it with simplicity..."
Romans 12:8 KJV

The Word of God says: *'So we, being many, are one body in Christ, and every one members one of another. Having then gifts differing according to the grace that is given to us, whether prophecy, let us prophesy according to the proportion of faith; Or ministry, let us wait on our ministering: or he that teacheth, on teaching; Or he that exhorteth, on exhortation: he that giveth, let him do it with simplicity; he that ruleth, with diligence; he that sheweth mercy, with cheerfulness.'* - Romans 12:5-8 KJV.

Friends, there is nothing complicated about the Word of God and the work of God: ministry. If we take the Word of God as TRUE and we minister ONLY with the grace He provides, we will be the most fulfilled people on earth.

What has the Lord commissioned you to do? Don't get it twisted. Do it with SIMPLICITY. That's how God gets to take the glory and you in turn don't get burnt out in the process.

"...let no man glory in men..."
1 Corinthians 3:21 KJV

You may have a very great family connection.

You may have great friends in high places who could get you whatever you want at a moment's notice.

You may even have powerful business partners who make things happen for you in your industry.

You are highly connected.

Good for you.

But the Word of God says you are not to glory in them. That is, they should never be your reason for confident boasting. If you must boast at all, you are to boast in God alone and in all He can do. God sees putting confidence in mere mortals as idolatry. He alone deserves your COMPLETE CONFIDENCE.

"Let every one of us please his neighbour for his good to edification. For even Christ pleased not himself..."
Romans 15:2-3 KJV

As Christians, we are not called to just do whatever seems good for us. Rather, we are called to do things that are in the best interest of others as well.

Jesus didn't live on earth to please Himself; else He wouldn't have gone through that terrible and excruciating death on the cross. Let's consider what is good for others in our dealings as God's children. That's His expectation from us.

"Let love be without dissimulation. Abhor that which is evil; cleave to that which is good"
Romans 12:9 KJV

The Word of God says we should love without dissimulation. What then is dissimulation? It means concealment of one's thoughts, feelings, or character; pretense.

God wants us to demonstrate our love for people by expressing it; He wants us to show it in our words, action, attitude, character, and the likes; until the recipients know without any doubt that they are loved. Someone has said: 'Love isn't yet love until it is expressed.' *Let love be without dissimulation...* And also remember to avoid evil, but cleave to what is good.

"...Let us destroy the tree with the fruit thereof..."
Jeremiah 11:19 KJV

Consider these words of Jesus in Matthew 7:17-19 KJV: *'Even so every good tree bringeth forth good fruit; but a corrupt tree bringeth forth evil fruit. A good tree cannot bring forth evil fruit, neither can a corrupt tree bring forth good fruit. Every tree that bringeth not forth good fruit is hewn down, and cast into the fire.'*

A bad tree cannot produce good fruits. If you live in the flesh, you will produce Galatians 5:19-21 (bad fruits); but if you live in the spirit, you will produce Galatians 5:22-23 (good fruits). So, to get rid of these bad fruits, you must destroy the tree producing them - the flesh (Galatians 5:24). That's why Apostle Paul declared the crucifixion (death) of his own flesh in Galatians 2:20 so he could get rid of its fruits. Want to get rid of bad fruits as well? Crucify the tree - your flesh.

"Let us therefore follow after the things which make for peace, and things wherewith one may edify another."
Romans 14:19 KJV

To follow after the things that make for peace doesn't require a special anointing. All it takes is to just do it. *'Let us follow...'* implies we can do it.

So, don't just look for things to argue about when discussing with people. Don't twist people's words and don't attack people verbally just because their beliefs are different from yours. Look for common grounds and work towards living at peace with everyone around you - in church, workplace, business place, family, etc.

Now, don't compromise your faith in Jesus just for peace's sake; that's not what God is saying. Rather, He's saying because of your relationship and connection with Jesus, be at peace with those around you.

"Let these sayings sink down into your ears..."
Luke 9:44 KJV

The words of Jesus are not just for preaching, teaching, or quoting. They call for serious and deep reflection. Why? Every word He speaks has a purpose, and it is in allowing them to sink down through conscious meditation that we access the deep truths they convey.

Don't just quote scriptures; allow the scriptures to *SINK DOWN INTO YOUR EARS*. That's how to convert logos to rhema for impact.

"...let every man take heed how he buildeth thereupon. For other foundation can no man lay than that is laid, which is Jesus Christ."
1 Corinthians 3:10-11 KJV

Jesus Christ is the Foundation of the Christian faith. He's the Author and Finisher of our faith, and everything else we do can only be regarded as building on the already laid foundation.

Now, all our preaching, teaching, and other works of ministry MUST reflect and conform with Christ - the Foundation. That's the only way those services will be acceptable and rewarded.

If what we build doesn't reflect Jesus - the Foundation, they will all be consumed by fire, and that simply implies fruitless labor - 1 Corinthians 3:12-15 KJV. How are you building on this Foundation?

"...let thy widows trust in me."
Jeremiah 49:11 KJV

The Word of God says *'Leave thy fatherless children, I will preserve them alive; and let thy widows trust in me.'* To be a widow isn't fun at all; especially in cultures where a woman's dignity is tied to her husbands' image and status.

Being a widow especially with young fatherless children, all the responsibilities of parenting literally fall on her, and that can be quite overwhelming.

However, there is good news. The Husband of all widows and the Father of the fatherless - the Almighty God - never leaves His widows to bear their burdens alone. In fact, He does the job better than anyone else on earth. So, are you widowed? Do not be afraid. Also, do not put your trust in uncles, aunts, in-laws, concerned friends, family members, etc. Accept their help and appreciate them, BUT PUT YOUR TRUST IN GOD ALONE. He never fails and He never disappoints. He will take care of you beyond your wildest imagination; and if you have children, He will raise them for you (Psalm 68:5). *Let thy widows trust in me...*

"...let him remember..."
Ecclesiastes 11:8 KJV

In this life, there are things the Lord wants us to remember. He wants us to remember them because it is very easy to forget about them.

For instance; *He wants us to remember that no sinner shall go unpunished; unless they repent. He wants us to remember that our time on earth is just like vapor; disappearing as fast as they appear. He wants us to remember that whatever we sow we shall reap; either good or bad. He wants us to remember that money, fame, social status and political power cannot help us on the day of death. He wants us to remember that no matter what we may be facing, His love is always surrounding us. He wants us to remember that no matter how beautiful our plans are, His plans for us are always better.* These are just to mention a few. What do you think the Lord wants you to remember today?

"Let us go early..."
Song of Songs 7:12 NIV

'Early' hardly goes wrong; *'Late'* is usually the problem. The Word of God says *'let us go early...'*

I know some cultures treat lateness so lightly. Even some government officials don't see anything wrong with being late to events.

However, as God's children, we are expected to shine as light in this dark world. We are not the ones who should be seen as late-comers, even in casual events. Being early also has its advantages. For instance, you could get some benefits that may become unavailable for late-comers.

Some people have been told things like *'we would have given it to you if you had arrived early; but now, it's finished.'* That's not the kind of statements early-comers get. Go early to God's Presence; Go early to work; Go early to appointments; Go early to meetings etc. If not for any other reason, GO EARLY because God's Word says so.

"...let thy heart cheer thee..."
Ecclesiastes 11:9 KJV

Being cheerful is more of a matter of the heart than the mind. The mind is exposed to tons of activities and distractions; thus, you may not be able to depend on it for joy.

As a Christian, your heart is God's dwelling place and His Presence is the generator of joy - the reason for seeing *'the joy of the Lord'* in the Bible. Let your heart be in tune with God regardless of what your mind is busy with. That's one sure way to *let thy heart cheer thee.*

"...Let him make speed, and hasten..."
Isaiah 5:19 KJV

Isn't it ironic that most people expect God to fulfill His promises in their lives speedily (without delay) while they delay in fulfilling theirs to Him?

God is never late, yet people still expect Him to move faster regarding their cases. In the same way you expect speed from God, He also expects speed from you.

He wants you to confess your sins to Him without delay so as to obtain forgiveness; He wants you to obey His commands speedily; He wants you to pay your vows speedily; He wants you to help people without hesitation; He wants you to fulfill your promises to Him and others without delay.

Whatever a man sows, that he shall also reap. Begin to obey God speedily and He will not delay the fulfillment of His promises in your life. SELAH!

"...let me see thy vengeance on them..."
Jeremiah 11:20 KJV

The Word of God says *'But, O LORD of hosts, that judgest righteously, that triest the reins and the heart, let me see thy vengeance on them: for unto thee have I revealed my cause'*.

Whenever we are hurt, it's a very natural tendency for us to try and hit back at our offenders. Some have even said *'vengeance is very sweet, especially when served cold.'* Why? Because you feel you have paid your offenders back in their own coin.

However, as far as God is concerned, He alone reserves the right to execute vengeance. He doesn't want any of His children to practice revenge. He wants us to commit our cause to Him and trust Him to carry out the necessary judgment.

So, whenever you are tempted to take revenge on some wrong done to you; remember that He's the only One Who does that. Just pray and ask Him to avenge you if you so much desire to see vengeance carried out. Do it God's way; He does it better than anyone else - including you.

"...let us declare in Zion the work of the LORD our God."
Jeremiah 51:10 KJV

Zion is God's dwelling place. And in our modern language, you could refer to a place of worship as Zion - that is, a church. Now, our text says *let us declare in Zion the work of the LORD our God*. That's what we should be doing in church.

When you go to church on Sundays or whatever day you meet for service, that's not the time to discuss politics, sports, some neighbors' marital challenges, some grievances experienced at work, some gossiping about a new member's mode of dressing, etc. Rather, you are expected to share testimonies of God's goodness in the past week, month, etc. You are to share with your fellow church members how you trusted God regarding a challenge and it was solved or how you prayed and God healed you.

That's what we do in Zion; not gossiping. What do you talk about when you go to church?

"...let me have joy of thee in the Lord..."
Philemon 1:20 KJV

Nothing gives spiritual parents (mentors) greater joy than seeing their spiritual children (mentees) walk in the spirit - living a Word-led life.

If you listen to your spiritual mentors but do not practice what you are taught, you are not giving them joy. It will appear as if their labor over your life is in vain.

They may not tell you to your face, but in their hearts, they are grieving over your life. God has provided us with great mentors in the Body of Christ. Some we are privileged to relate with directly, while others we are only able to relate with indirectly. But either way, the Lord wants us to give our spiritual mentors joy by living out what they teach us and what we see them do - all to the glory of God alone.

Hebrews 13:17 KJV says: *'Obey them that have the rule over you, and submit yourselves: for they watch for your souls, as they that must give account, that they may do it with joy, and not with grief: for that is unprofitable for you.'* Today, decide to let your spiritual leaders *'have joy of thee in the Lord'*.

"...let us sing unto the LORD..."
Psalm 95:1 KJV

Humans are singing creatures. We sing when alone, we sing in groups, we sing at events, and we sing for different reasons. We sing at naming ceremonies and we even sing at funerals. We are singing beings.

However, in our text today the Psalmist is encouraging us to *sing unto the LORD*. Why? Because God loves to hear His children sing to Him. So, go ahead and compose nice songs and sing to His glory. If you can't compose, sing songs from worship leaders and just glorify the Lord with them.

Let your voice not be used to sing for the devil: don't sing immoral songs in clubs and pubs; don't sing unto idols during your village's fetish festivals; don't use your God-given voice to sing songs that do not glorify God. Even in church, don't just sing to entertain the audience; sing your songs *UNTO THE LORD!*

"Let them alone: they be blind leaders of the blind. And if the blind lead the blind, both shall fall into the ditch."
Matthew 15:14 KJV

When it comes to leaders or ministers who are too blind by religion to see the reality of life in the spirit, *LET THEM ALONE*. Don't attend their programs, don't listen to their messages, and don't follow them. You may pray for them from afar, but don't be close to them.

Do you know why? Jesus said they are headed for the ditch (unless they repent of course); and if you are in their company, you won't be able to escape the ditch either. *Let them alone!*

"...let him impart to him that hath none..."
Luke 3:11 KJV

One of the reasons the Lord blesses us is to be able to pass it on. God delights in using His people to bless others. For instance, your ability to teach may be God's way of bringing understanding to those who are deficient in knowledge. Also, your salary raise may be God's way of providing for those in lack (through you).

There is something you have that is lacking in others. Fill the gap. Meet the need. Engage your prayers, expertise, talent, abilities, resources, etc. You know you have it; now *'impart to him that hath none...'.* Your reward shall be great. Trust me.

"...let us plead together..."
Isaiah 43:26 KJV

Has it ever occurred to you that you could actually discuss with God? Yeah. You can discuss any subject matter with Him. According to our text, He's even the One inviting you to come and plead with Him.

So, is there anything happening in your life or around you that you are not comfortable with? Go ahead and discuss it with Him. You notice no matter how hard you try, you keep falling into temptations. You keep doing what you have promised yourself over and over again to not do; it's high time you discussed it with Him.

Tell Him how it feels, tell Him how much you have tried; and of course, tell Him to help you. Share your weaknesses with Him and ask Him for a strategy to help you overcome them. Discuss it with the Lord; He's waiting to hear from you.

"...Let not the wise man glory in his wisdom, neither let the mighty man glory in his might, let not the rich man glory in his riches: But let him that glorieth glory in this, that he understandeth and knoweth me, that I am the LORD which exercise lovingkindness, judgment, and righteousness, in the earth: for in these things I delight, saith the LORD."
Jeremiah 9:23-24 KJV

Those verses were directly from the mouth of the Lord: *'Thus saith the LORD'* was the opening statement. God doesn't want any of us to boast about our wisdom, achievements, skills, status, etc.

Rather, He wants us to boast of our relationship with Him and our knowledge of Him. That's the only kind of boasting that is acceptable to Him. He practically takes delight in such. Think about that!

"...let him declare what he seeth."
Isaiah 21:6 KJV

Being a witness is a very great responsibility; your testimony could determine who dies and who lives. It could determine who gets condemned and who gets justified.

Whenever you are called upon to give a testimony regarding an event or a case, decide to only say what you know, heard, or saw. That's the kind of witnessing that God expects. Nothing but the absolute truth!

Even when it comes to evangelism (witnessing for Jesus); learn to declare what you see in His Word. Only His Word can save sinners; not your eloquent speech or untrue stories. *LET HIM DECLARE WHAT HE SEETH...*

"...let him declare what he seeth."
Isaiah 21:6 KJV

When God shows you something through His Word or visions regarding your family, church members, co-workers, etc, especially as a warning, it's your responsibility to declare what you see so they can be aware and take necessary action.

In Acts 27:22-44, there was trouble at sea; but Paul declared what he saw and heard, and the people were encouraged. And sure enough, no soul was lost as the Lord had promised him. If you don't declare, someone might end up making an avoidable mistake or simply end up committing suicide whereas they could have been encouraged by the declaration of what you were shown. *Let him declare what he seeth...*

"...let him declare what he seeth."
Isaiah 21:6 KJV

When God shows you a revelation or something not visible to others; it's a privilege. And He doesn't show people things just so they may feel good. He shows these things for specific purposes.

It is however written in His Word that until you begin to declare these things you have been shown, they may never come to pass in your life. Jesus said *'ye shall have whatever ye say'* (Mark 11:23).

If God shows you that He is opening a great door of opportunity for you, He wants you to start declaring it with your mouth. To Him, declaring it means you believe it and you're expecting it (2 Corinthians 4:13). When God shows you these things, learn to declare them; and you shall have them manifest in your life.

He said by His stripes you were healed; learn to declare that whenever you feel sickness is knocking. *Let him declare what he seeth...*

"...let them stretch forth the curtains of thine habitations: spare not, lengthen thy cords, and strengthen thy stakes; For thou shalt break forth on the right hand and on the left..."

Isaiah 54:2-3 KJV

The God we serve is famous for declaring the end right from the beginning. He calls those things that be not as though they were.

Now, when such a God gives you a promise, you can count on His integrity to bring it to pass. So, even before you see the manifestation, you can start making arrangements to receive them.

For instance, as a barren woman with the promise of fruitfulness, you can begin to set up your baby crib, get baby things, etc. That's how to prepare for what's coming. Our text implies making room to receive what God is bringing. That is believing God and expecting Him to do what He has promised.

"...Let the LORD be glorified..."
Isaiah 66:5 KJV

Giving God the glory isn't a passive affair. It's a very conscious decision and an active expression. For instance, as a child of God, when someone offends you, you have two options: glorify God or deny Him the glory. If you take matters into your own hands and you retaliate or take vengeance on the wrong done to you, you have simply chosen to glorify yourself and dishonor God. However, if you choose to let it go and let God handle it the best way He feels, you have chosen to glorify Him.

In every conversation, transaction, event, project, financial decision among other things that characterize our daily lives, we will always have the opportunity to choose whom we will glorify - ourselves, our bosses, our spouses, our relatives, our friends, our political leaders, our spiritual leaders OR THE ALMIGHTY GOD. But as for me and my household, we will glorify the Lord. What about you?

"...Let us go again and visit our brethren in every city where we have preached the word of the Lord, and see how they do."
Acts 15:36 KJV

Being born again is one thing, but being established in the faith is another thing. To be saved, you need an encounter with the Saviour. But to become an established and devoted follower of Jesus, you need nurturing. And that's where discipleship comes in.

For those of us involved in the Great Commission; thank you so much for depleting the kingdom of darkness and bringing souls into the eternal life that can only be found in Christ Jesus.

However, that's just the beginning. We still need to follow these souls up and help them know the Lord better so they can become established. Apostle Paul said to visit them again. And that's a good way to go about it. But because we are so blessed now with technology, we can also use phone calls, text messages, social media interactions, virtual meetings, etc to reach out to these blessed ones.

Don't just win these souls to the Lord; pray for them daily and as much as you can, follow up on them until they become established in the faith. Remember, the devil doesn't give up on anyone. Don't leave them alone, please. God bless your heart!

"Let no man deceive himself. If any man among you seemeth to be wise in this world, let him become a fool, that he may be wise. For the wisdom of this world is foolishness with God..."
1 Corinthians 3:18-19 KJV

The worst thing that can happen to a man is to be caught up in self-deception. To deceive others is bad enough; but when you begin to deceive yourself, it's another level entirely.

You know what the will of God is but you pretend and act as if you don't know. Who are you deceiving? The Word of God says to become wise in God's sight, you have to become foolish (in the sight of the world). This is because the highest level of wisdom on earth is absolute foolishness as far as God is concerned.

Building up your resume with fake certificates and false qualifications may appear smart and even get you a job. But that's deception, and you know it. Become a *'fool'* as far as this worldly system is concerned, so you can become WISE with God.

"...let him be unto thee as an heathen man ..."
Matthew 18:17 KJV

Jesus said in Matthew 18:15-17 *'Moreover if thy brother shall trespass against thee, go and tell him his fault between thee and him alone: if he shall hear thee, thou hast gained thy brother. But if he will not hear thee, then take with thee one or two more, that in the mouth of two or three witnesses every word may be established. And if he shall neglect to hear them, tell it unto the church: but if he neglect to hear the church, let him be unto thee as an heathen man and a publican.'*

This is the FORMULA for CONFLICT RESOLUTION IN THE BODY OF CHRIST AS INSTITUTED BY THE HEAD OF THE CHURCH HIMSELF- JESUS CHRIST.

Do this; and if it fails, do what Jesus said. Treat the offender as an unbeliever. Love them, but don't be unequally yoked with them. That is, don't have a brotherhood relationship with them. That way, you won't lose your peace.

"Let them praise his name in the dance: let them sing praises unto him with the timbrel and harp. For the LORD taketh pleasure in his people: he will beautify the meek with salvation."
Psalm 149:3-4 KJV

I don't know where you worship; but if dancing has been painted as an expression of carnality in your church, I'm afraid they haven't read the Bible well enough. Dancing to the Lord is a form of praise that is highly acceptable to Him. He takes pleasure and delight in seeing His children dance.

Let's say you have a very cheerful child who always sings and dances, will you be sad as a good parent? Of course not. But if that child is always gloomy and complaining, you will definitely not be happy. Dancing to the Lord is an expression of joy because you can't be sad and be dancing; and as the BEST PARENT ALIVE, God is very happy when you are happy. Go ahead and praise the Lord in a dance, you are not being carnal.

"...let him that speaketh in an unknown tongue pray that he may interpret."
1 Corinthians 14:13 KJV

As beautiful as speaking in an unknown tongue is, especially for those who know its purpose and benefits, it may also generate confusion in our assemblies.

Speaking in an unknown tongue may edify you, fine-tune your spirit-man and even guide you into praying correctly; but when you begin to run your church services entirely on tongues, you are missing the whole point.

God wants His Church to be edified (built-up); so, He would rather have you minister to your congregation prophetically in a way they would understand than see you blast off in tongues.

If you (or anyone) in your congregation must deliver a message in tongues, the Word of God says such a fellow should pray for the ability to interpret. Because it is in the interpretation that the church will be blessed. Ministers of God please take note!

"...Let them show it by their good life..."
James 3:13 NIV

The Word of God says *'Who is wise and understanding among you? Let them show it by their good life, by deeds done in the humility that comes from wisdom.'*

Your confession is empty without your corresponding actions. You can claim to be wise; but if your actions keep depicting folly, then that's your true state.

God wants your life to line up with your words. You say you are a man of integrity; prove it by the way you live. Someone has said *'talk is cheap, anyone can afford it.'* The Word of the Lord to you today is *'start walking the talk'*. Do good works with *the humility that comes from wisdom.*

"...let him go free."
Psalm 105:20 KJV

We give glory to God for the revelations He has brought us through this 'LET' Series. May His Name forever be praised in Jesus' Name. Now, as we conclude, the Lord wants you to do this without any delay: *RELEASE YOUR OFFENDERS; LET THEM GO FREE.*

Has anyone caused you any form of pain in the course of your life? *LET THEM GO FREE!* Has anyone disappointed you lately? *LET THEM GO FREE!* Have you been assaulted by someone at work? *LET THEM GO FREE!* Are you a victim of sexual or drug abuse, with the thought of revenge on the offender playing in your head? *LET THEM GO FREE!* Who do you still have bitterness and resentment towards? *LET THEM GO FREE!*

You don't want to carry any unnecessary baggage into the remaining glorious years of your life. For Christ's sake (not for the offenders' sake), *RELEASE THEM IN YOUR HEART AND THE LORD WILL HEAL YOUR EMOTIONAL WOUNDS.*

God bless your heart in Jesus' Name.

WHY YOU REALLY NEED JESUS!

You might have heard a lot of Preachers talk about the importance of surrendering one's life to Jesus and even the dangers of not doing so at one time or the other without you being really moved. But with these three (3) important reasons highlighted below, I strongly believe you will not need another sermon before deciding to yield to His saving grace regardless of your religious beliefs.

1. **You have an Enemy to overcome:** There is an adversary who is all out to steal from you, kill you and destroy you regardless of your level of education, moral uprightness, societal influence or even religious beliefs. He is Devil by name (John 10:10, 1 Peter 5: 8), and he doesn't release any of his captives until he completely destroys their souls in hell. The ONLY One Who can deliver you from his manipulations and also save your soul from him is Jesus Christ.
2. **You have an Appointment to keep:** Being alive and reading this implies you have a very important and inevitable appointment to keep. It is an appointment with death (Hebrews 9:27). Death is the sure end of all mortals (of which you are part); and to enable you prepare for this appointment without fear of eternal damnation, you need Jesus. He is the ONLY One Who has power over death (Revelation 1:18).
3. **You have a Judge to face:** Upon departure from this earth, you will have to stand before a judgment throne to render an account of your earthly life (Hebrews 9:27, Romans 14:12). The outcome of this judgment is what will determine your eternal abode which will either be Heaven or the Lake of fire. Interestingly, the Judge Who will preside over your case and also decide where you will spend your eternity is Jesus (John 5:21-30, 2 Timothy 4:1). I perceive you are thinking "is God not our Judge? Why Jesus?' Well, you are not wrong. But God the Father Himself is the One Who handed over all the judgment to His Son, Jesus Christ. Read the verse 22 of that John chapter 5. So, Jesus is the ONLY One Who has the power to either judge you guilty or guiltless in eternity.

Now that you know these, the wisest thing you can do for yourself is to quickly establish a relationship with Jesus, since you don't even know how close your appointment with death is. To do this, say this prayer aloud: *"Lord Jesus, I am a sinner and I cannot help myself. Wash me in your precious blood and make me a new creature. I open the door of my heart to you today, come into my life and become my Lord and Savior. Grant me the grace to overcome the devil, prepare me for eternity and help me to escape the judgment reserved for sinners. Thank You Jesus for saving me. Amen."*

Congratulations! You are now SAVED. Go and sin no more. To learn more about your new relationship with Jesus, kindly send an email to info@gloem.org and we will send you a material that will help you. You can also call, text or send WhatsApp message to +1 587 9735910 or +1 587 9695910 for further assistance.

And to learn more about God, His Word and His plans for your life, kindly like our Facebook page *@gloem.org* for daily meditation of the Word of God (all year round) and visit our Blog page [*https://gloem.org/my-blog*] for life transforming publications.

You are also invited to listen to GLOEM Podcast every Monday via https://anchor.fm/gloem All these great resources that are capable of developing your spiritual stamina will help you become an overcomer in life regardless of what comes your way.

ABOUT THE AUTHOR

By the special grace of God, **Anthony O. Adefarakan** is the privileged President of **Global Emancipation Ministries - Calgary (GLOEM)** with headquarters in Canada, North America and **Emancipating Truth Ministry International (ETMI)** with headquarters in Nigeria, West Africa.

The Lord called him into the field ministry in February 2008 with the mandate to liberate men through the knowledge of the Truth, and by December 2012 he was ordained and commissioned as the Pioneer Pastor – in – Charge of The Redeemed Christian Church of God, Revelation Parish, Shalom Area under Delta Province III, Nigeria where he served until 1st February 2015 when he officially handed over to a new Pastor in order to focus on his field ministry to which the Lord had earlier called him and for which the authority of the church had already prayed and released him to undertake.

On 29th September 2013, he was awarded a Post Graduate Diploma in Tent – Making Mission from the Redeemed Christian School of Missions, Nigeria (RECSOM, Asaba Campus) where he also had the privilege to train Pastors and Missionaries as a lecturer in 2017.

Since the commissioning of his field ministry in 2015 he has had the opportunity to lead his ministry officers to field ministrations in different Prisons, Hospitals, Orphanages, Rural communities, Camp settlements, Markets, Local churches among other places with great successes on all occasions – such as salvation of sinners, healing of the sick, financial empowerment of mission churches, provision of relief materials to the poor, provision of medical services to the under-privileged, baptism in the Holy Ghost, deliverance from demonic oppression, release of inmates just to mention a few - all to the glory of God Who alone is the Doer.

He is the author of other best-selling titles such as ***The Law of Kinds, It's Your Size, The Immutability of God's Counsel, Surely there is an End, Life Applicable lessons from the Book of Ruth, One thing is Needful, Life Applicable Revelations from God's Word*** among others. He is happily married to Ifeoluwa A. Adefarakan and their marriage is fruitful to the glory of God. **Jesus is his Message, Freedom is the Outcome! Isaiah 61:1-3.**

www.gloem.org

BECOME A FINANCIAL PARTNER WITH JESUS

At *Global Emancipation Ministries - Calgary*, our mandate is *to liberate men through the knowledge of the Truth* and our mission statement is *creating channels through which men can encounter the Truth - Isaiah 61:1-3; John 8:32, 36; I Thessalonians 5:24.*

Our Ministerial Activities include Rural and Urban Evangelical Outreaches, Prison Evangelism, Hospital Ministrations, Mobilization for Missions Support, Teaching of the undiluted Word of God, Scripture-Based Seminars, Discipleship, Training of Field Missionaries and Empowerment of underprivileged ones among other Field Ministerial Tasks.

If you sense the Lord is calling you to reach out to the lost by engaging in any of these activities or by assisting those involved with your resources, please feel free to join us. Let us come together as we take the Gospel of our Lord Jesus Christ to the hurting and forgotten ones. [Mark 16:15-20].

Please join us in these kingdom projects by making your weekly, monthly, quarterly or annual donations to: Global Emancipation Ministries – Calgary, **TD Canada Trust (TD Bank), 5247676**

You can also visit the "GIVE" section on our website, www.gloem.org, to learn about other ways to give. For acknowledgement, please advise your donations to us by email: info@gloem.org, and kindly include your details i.e. name, address, email and location. Alternatively, you can simply call +1 587 9735910 to do same.

You can also volunteer your gifts and talents in the service of the Lord through our ministerial platforms regardless of your location. To get information on how to go about this, please visit www.gloem.org or send us an email via info@gloem.org.

God bless you.

OTHER TITLES BY THE AUTHOR AND HIS WIFE

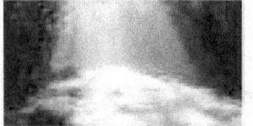

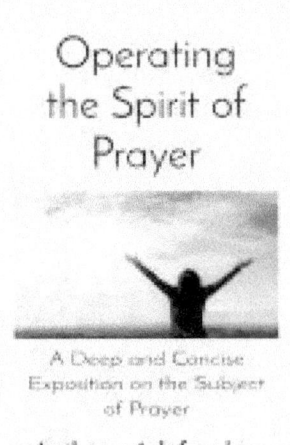

THE "LET" SERIES | 139

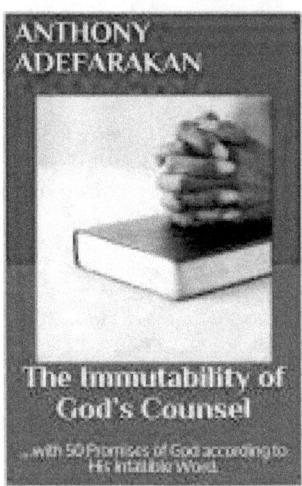

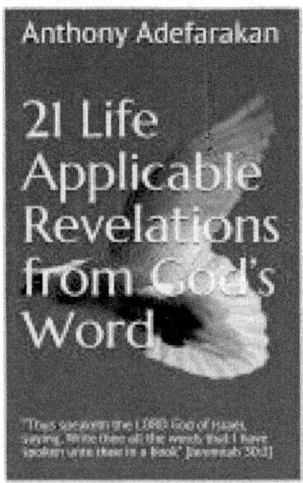

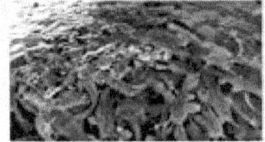

50 FREQUENTLY ASKED QUESTIONS BY FISH FARMERS WITH DETAILED ANSWERS

ANTHONY ADEFARAKAN

Scan the QR Codes below to access these titles

www.ingramcontent.com/pod-product-compliance
Lightning Source LLC
Chambersburg PA
CBHW081146060526
44107CB00135B/710